BEFORE YOU SAY
'I DO'

relate

BEFORE YOU SAY
'I DO'

How To Be
Happily Married For Ever!

Elizabeth Martyn

Vermilion
LONDON

First published in the United Kingdom in 2003 by Vermilion
an imprint of Ebury Press
Random House UK Limited
Random House · 20 Vauxhall Bridge Road · London SW1V 2SA

Random House Australia (Pty) Limited
20 Alfred Street · Milsons Point · Sydney · New South Wales 2061 · Australia

Random House New Zealand Limited
18 Poland Road · Glenfield · Auckland 10 · New Zealand

Random House (Pty) Limited
Endulini · 5A Jubilee Road · Parktown 2193 · South Africa

Random House UK Limited Reg. No. 954009

www.randomhouse.co.uk

Papers used by Vermilion are natural, recyclable products made
from wood grown in sustainable forests.

A CIP catalogue record is available for this book from the British Library.

ISBN: 0 09 188458 6

Text design by Lovelock & Co.

Printed and bound in Great Britain by Bookmarque Ltd · Croydon · Surrey

Contents

Acknowledgements

A warm thank you to all the many people who took the time to advise and encourage me in the writing of this book.

To all those at Relate, who gave generously of their time and expertise, including Gill Bolt, Ruth Cole, Paula Hall, Evie Hughes, Irene Hunt, Charlotte Imbert, Denise Knowles, Shoina Lloyd, Kate Maycock, John O'Reilly, Angela Sibson, Jill Sylvester, Andrew Tyler and Annie Wilson. I am especially grateful to Christine Northam for her invaluable contributions to the book.

Thank you also to fellow writers Julia Cole and Susan Quilliam, my agent Charlotte Howard, and Jacqueline Burns and Lesley McOwan at Vermilion for the support and encouragement you have given me.

Very special thanks are due to all those who talked to me so openly about their experiences of marriage, and allowed me to quote them. Your honesty and insights have greatly enriched the book.

And lastly, thanks to my husband Tony – for everything.

About Relate

Relate – The Relationship People

Relate works with people to help them make their relationships better. We help people understand themselves better, make sense of their relationships and decide what they want to do. The different ways Relate can help means there will be a Relate service right for you.

Relationship counselling helps couples and individuals who want to work through a problem. You can meet with a Relate counsellor face-to-face by contacting your local Relate Centre, or have sessions with your counsellor on the phone.

Sex therapy is available at Relate Centres nationwide for couples or individuals with specific sex problems, such as lack of desire or impotence. Relate is the largest provider of couple counselling and sex therapy in the UK.

Relate family counselling can help when relationships at home between family members hit a problem. It may be sibling feuds, communication breakdown with teenagers, or resentments within a stepfamily.

Learning about relationship skills and understanding yourself better can often prevent problems arising in the first place. Relate runs a variety of **courses** on subjects, ranging from commitment for couples (see page 9) to anger management, as well as one for the newly single.

Relate works to support relationships in the home and at work.

We run courses and can develop programmes for employers to support their staff. We also work with young people individually and through schools.

The Relate website offers some **advice on common problems**, or you can submit your own personal query to our Relate Online **consulting service** and get a personal reply. There are Relate Centres across the UK. Use our website to find the one nearest to you.

Relate also publishes many other useful books on many aspects of relationships. See page 197 for details.

Contact Relate on: 0845 456 1310
www.relate.org.uk

The Relate Couples Course

Relate has years of experience as the relationship experts. We know that couples who take the time to explore their relationship and who have begun to develop their communication skills together start their married life on a good footing.

Reading this book is a good start for any couple about to get married, getting them on the right path for developing a strong and committed relationship. Relate also offers a Couples Course, which is relevant to today's lifestyles and it is aimed at any couple entering into a commitment together, whether that is marriage, living together or starting a family. This short course covers areas such as communication, conflict, commitment, money, sex and personal expectations and fulfilment. It is a useful way to get both partners thinking and talking together.

Relate courses are run locally around the UK. For information on where the Couples Course is running, or to find out how to arrange one in your community, please visit the Relate website www.relate.org.uk or call 0845 456 1310.

Introduction

What Makes a Marriage Work?

A wedding is a moment of supreme hope and optimism. How wonderful to find the person you want to share your life with. How exciting to set out on a shared journey together. At the same time, though, comes the question: how can a couple avoid the much-quoted divorce statistics and enjoy a marriage that flourishes into the long-distance future?

A happy and stable marriage is something that people yearn for. A love that lasts a lifetime is immensely desirable, quite apart from the fact that research shows married people to be better off, healthier and less prone to depression. So what are the secrets of getting it quietly but consistently right?

Married couples don't fall into neat categories. Couples are so different, expectations so wide-ranging. One couple might long for a family of five, another might decide not to have kids at all. Marriage could involve the mingling of two cultures, or the blending of two families of children. You might be tying the knot with your first true love, or entering into a new marriage after the traumas of a divorce. Whatever your age and stage of life, whatever your situation, your hopes and dreams for marriage are unique. This book will help you to reflect on that unique relationship and work out your own definition of a successful, happy marriage.

What your marriage looks like, how you play it out day by day, is highly personal and different in every relationship. Even so, there are elements that Relate counsellors identify as being important to enrich a marriage and keep it alive and vibrant. In good marriages, you can expect to find love and respect, warmth and tenderness, laughter, harmony, fidelity, satisfying sex, pleasurable companionship, mutual acceptance, a spark of electricity, an element of the unpredictable. Couples whose marriages last well know how to communicate and compromise, can sort out their differences, and accept and value each other, warts and all. They laugh together, spend enough time together, and put each other first whenever they can. They know it won't all be plain sailing, but they're prepared to take the rough along with the smooth.

When a marriage is happy and fulfilling, it's wonderful. When a marriage goes wrong, the misery can be overwhelming. That's why it is worth putting in effort and thought, never taking it for granted. Marriage does take time, compromise and a lot else, but the rewards are great: a relationship that lasts a lifetime, bringing happiness and fun, laughter and pleasure, a shoulder to lean on in good times and bad, and an underpinning of love to enrich and enhance the rest of your life.

'Why our marriage works'

'My husband and I have been married for 44 years. He is my best friend and I am his. When there is anything to discuss, he is my first choice. We love being together, even if it's driving and not saying a word for miles.' MARIA, MARRIED TO JOHN

'It's not like anything you see on TV. We've gone through some horrendous times. But I feel ridiculously proud and happy that we've reached our 25th anniversary.' TIM, MARRIED TO KAY

'If I learned anything at all from my first marriage, it's that you can't short-change your partner on talk. Claire and I make a special effort to have regular time together, and are always open about our feelings.' JONATHAN

'To me, marriage means there's an underpinning to my life. I see our two lives becoming more intertwined in every way – socially, emotionally and financially. It's rather like constructing a house. As each year passes, we're adding more building blocks to the walls. There are doors in the house giving us freedom to go in and out and enjoy our own interests and hobbies. But together inside, it's a place of refuge and security.' LIZ, MARRIED FOR 23 YEARS TO PETER

'We got married eight years ago, and the real reason was so that he could stay in this country. Without that, we'd have gone on living together. I never thought I'd feel this, but I really love being married, I'm proud to wear the ring that Bertrand gave me. Marriage has made a real difference to both of us. We're together for keeps now. It's a good feeling.' ADELE

'Having the children together has been fantastic, despite the times I thought I'd sink when they were tiny. It's lovely doing the mum and dad thing. But – and this is the important bit – it's still fantastic being together without them. It's such a treat when they're off playing with friends and we can have a proper chat over a glass of wine. Love it.' RUKHSANA MARRIED FOR 12 YEARS TO DAVE

'Sexiness wears thin after a while, and beauty fades. But to be married to a man who makes you laugh every day, ah, now that's a treat.' JOANNE WOODWARD, MARRIED TO ACTOR PAUL NEWMAN

'What makes our marriage happy is that we both feel we can be ourselves, there's no pretending. Making the binding commitment of marriage was very important, and helps us feel that we can trust in our love for each other, whatever happens.' IAN, MARRIED FOR 15 YEARS TO DEBBIE

'The entrancing gossip of bedroom life, the crackles of annoyance, the candlelit battleground, the truces, the fun, the love, the rage. In marriage there are no manners to keep up, and beneath the wildest accusations no real criticism.' ENID BAGNOLD, NOVELIST

'There have been times when a huge gulf has opened up – after the children were born were the worst times – and we've lived side by side for months at a time more like siblings than spouses. Underneath, though, there's a strong bond, and so the tide always turns – I guess we make it turn – and we get closer together again.' JAMES, MARRIED FOR 11 YEARS TO TAMAR

'Marriage to me is the richest reward of life this side of heaven. The essence of true, lasting love is giving. It's a decision you make even when you don't 'feel' like it. It means looking out for your partner's interests before your own.' BARBIE, MARRIED FOR 32 YEARS TO PETER

'We've both been married before, and we've both learned a lot, the hard way. Now we know that you can't let things slide, if there's a problem you must talk it out, try and solve it, you've got to keep your sex life going, and make plans that involve each other. Plus you need to take on board each other's quirks. And you've got to have fun together, jokes, treats, that kind of thing. That's what's different this time – this marriage is so much fun.' FLORENCE, MARRIED FOR 5 YEARS TO ALEC

'If there is goodwill on both sides, no marriage need fail.' AMY, AGED 76, AND MARRIED FOR 50 YEARS TO JIM, WHO SAYS, 'Each year is better than the one before...'

1
Aim High

Getting married is a truly exciting beginning, the start of a whole lifetime of being together, loving each other, and building your future together. You're in love, everything feels right, and getting married sets the seal on your happiness and hopes.

With so much anticipation and trust invested in this, the most important relationship of your lives, it makes a lot of sense to check out each other's expectations. After all, if you were going somewhere new on holiday, you'd read the guidebooks. If you were starting a new job, you'd find out how the company worked. The same applies to getting married, the ultimate new experience, and one on which the whole of your joint future rests.

Ask yourself what you expect. Are your expectations high? Good. Marrying in a mood of shared optimism, with great plans

---

SPEAKING FROM EXPERIENCE

'To me, being married is about being in it for the long haul. From day to day we have our ups and downs, but we have decided that we will fight life's battles together. We've been married for 14 years now and we've found that real commitment means that we're stronger and happier than when we're on our own.' CHARLOTTE

---

for your future, gets you off to a brilliant start. It's really important, though, that from the outset you share the same wish-list. People often place huge demands on their marriage to cater for a mass of needs, both practical and emotional. As well as happiness, they dream of good sex for ever, financial stability, friendship, support and so on.

All those things are possible, but to have them you must both be willing to put in whatever it takes, even when the going gets rough as, over the years, it sometimes will. If one of you is less than wholehearted, or hasn't thought beyond the romance of the wedding to consider what the real-life experience of being married might involve, then your expectations will be mismatched, and someone's bound to end up disappointed.

Why Marry?

What people hope for from marriage is closely linked to their reasons for marrying. Before you start looking at what you want out of your marriage, think about why it is that you are getting married in the first place.

There are lots of reasons for marrying, some romantic, some prosaic. Counsellor Irene Hunt says, 'People marry for a partner, for companionship, for romance. On its own, being "in love" really isn't a good enough reason to marry. You need a lot of other things.'

Every decision to marry is fed by dozens of complicated needs and desires. For instance, some people marry because it feels like the right thing to do at their particular stage in life, whatever that might be. Or they marry for financial reasons, such as to avoid inheritance tax, or to give their partner rights to a pension. As long as pragmatic reasons like money or timing are part of a bigger picture and underpin a relationship that is emotionally viable and strong, then there's nothing wrong with them.

What are the less sound reasons for marrying? Anything that carries an unspoken emotional agenda is risky, such as wanting to pin the other partner down, shore up a failing relationship, or have a longed-for child even if your partner doesn't really want one. Reasons like these set the marriage off on a shaky footing.

THE BIG QUESTIONS

Why are we getting married?

Check through this list of reasons for marrying. Think about which apply to you, then reflect on them. Will your marriage be able to fulfil the needs behind your reasons for getting married? As with most exercises in the book, it's most fruitful to do this separately first, then check to see how closely your answers match.

Reasons for marrying

- Being in love. ☐ ☐
- To spend the rest of our lives together. ☐ ☐
- To make a public commitment. ☐ ☐
- To make a commitment within a religious
  ceremony. ☐ ☐
- To prove to everyone that I'm OK. ☐ ☐
- Marriage is the next step because we:
  - have been living together. ☐ ☐
  - have bought a house together. ☐ ☐
  - have a child or children together. ☐ ☐
  - are expecting our first child. ☐ ☐
  - want to have children within a marriage. ☐ ☐
- It's the right time. ☐ ☐

- Everyone else is getting married. ☐ ☐
- If we don't get married, we'll probably split up. ☐ ☐
- Getting married will solve our problems. ☐ ☐
- There are good financial/practical reasons
  for marrying. ☐ ☐
- To get back at an ex-partner. ☐ ☐
- Always dreamed of having a big wedding. ☐ ☐
- Got it wrong in my first marriage and want
  another chance. ☐ ☐
- Have children from previous relationship and want:
      to provide a secure home for them. ☐ ☐
      to provide a step-parent for them. ☐ ☐
- Afraid that no one else will have me. ☐ ☐
- Want my partner to make a commitment to me. ☐ ☐
- Enjoy each other's company. ☐ ☐
- Our families expect it. ☐ ☐
- Tired of coping as a single parent. ☐ ☐
- Want to escape from family. ☐ ☐
- Marriage is an important part of the culture
  to which one or both of us belong. ☐ ☐
- Can't manage without each other. ☐ ☐
- Don't want to be alone again. ☐ ☐

*This list is not exhaustive. Are there any other reasons why you
are getting married? Your hopes and needs from marriage should
be similar, and neither partner should feel pressurised into
marriage – it should definitely be a joint decision. Beware, too, of
snap decisions to marry – you might be lucky, but marriage is a
big commitment, and there's truth in the old saying 'Marry in
haste, repent at leisure'.*

The Wedding Day

A thriving industry has grown up around the business of getting
hitched. In the UK, the average white wedding, including an
exotic honeymoon, costs a staggering £13,000. Weddings are fun,
but they can take over your life and cause family ructions (see
page 160 on how to involve your family in your wedding plans
without them taking over).

*Two men bid the £250,000 reserve price asked in order to
marry Kay Hammond, 24, who auctioned herself on-line. A
spokeswoman said: "Kay plans to meet both of them, but if
all other things are equal, she is not bothered who she
marries and will choose the highest bidder."*

How do you view your wedding day? An excuse for a great party? One of the most important days of your life? Something worth spending lots and lots of money on?

There's nothing wrong with having a lavish wedding if that's what both of you want (note the 'both'). Plenty of couples throw themselves into the arrangements and create a memorable wedding enjoyed by everyone and remembered with pleasure for years to come. The danger lies if the wedding is an end in itself, or represents the living out of a fantasy that isn't backed up by genuine feelings.

Wedding dresses, for example, exotic creations, change a woman into someone she's never looked like before. If you're trying to act out a fantasy or turn yourself into someone else, stop and think: it's OK for your wedding to fulfil a childhood dream of being a beautiful bride, but it has to go beyond that. The frills are like the froth on a cappuccino – delicious, but gone in moments. What really counts is the ceremony and how you feel about it. Wedding celebrations last for a day or two. Marriage is for the rest of your life.

'Before we were married it was all so exciting.'

Sandy and Alec saved for two years for their wedding and honeymoon. Six months after they were married, they came to Relate. Sandy explained: 'Before we were married it was all so exciting, there was so much to think about and plan. But now we're short of money because we've taken on a mortgage and we're paying off the loan for the wedding. We're both working, but we're not working *towards* anything any more. I do love Alec, but we seem to bicker all the time – he doesn't want to help with stuff in the house, sex has gone right off – being married is just no fun.'

Counsellors say: *'When the wedding day itself becomes the goal, couples don't give any time to thinking about what they want from marriage. The woman and her family often do most of the work of planning the wedding, and the man gets left out. It's a treat for her – he just has to put his suit on and turn up. Once the honeymoon's over they both have to try and accept reality. It's a comedown from the big event.*

'Alec and Sandy need to sit down together and review their situation. Why are they feeling so flat? What did they expect from marriage that they're not getting? Then they can set up new goals for themselves, as a couple and as individuals. One way to do this is to take a big piece of paper and divide it into four squares. In the first, write down where you are now; in the second, think about where you want to be; in the third, ask yourselves what's stopping you getting there; and in the fourth, identify one small step you can take together to start making the change.'

The Honeymoon

Don't forget to check out your expectations of the honeymoon. Go easy on yourselves, especially if you're planning a big wedding. You don't want your holiday of a lifetime spoiled because:

- you're shattered after all the wedding preparations
- you've had a mega journey, or are trying to adjust to a different climate or very exotic surroundings
- there doesn't seem to be anything to talk about now that the wedding is over
- you're still coming down from all the excitement and the honeymoon feels like an anti-climax
- you feel the pressure of other people expecting you to be having a wonderful romantic holiday, with oodles of wild sex
- you're together 24/7 – something many couples aren't used to.

Keep these things in mind when you plan your honeymoon. Try to

---

SPEAKING FROM EXPERIENCE

'At the end of our wedding day, a friend drove us 30 miles away to a quiet country B&B, and we spent three nights there. Then we came home, went back to work, saw our wedding pictures, opened the presents and took things fairly easy – we were both feeling a bit frayed after the run-up to the wedding. Six weeks later we went on a three-week holiday round the Greek islands and it was great: we'd had a chance to recover from the wedding, we were really looking forward to a holiday, and by spreading things out like that we kept the feeling of celebration and the romantic bit going.' GEORGE

---

avoid jetting off immediately after the wedding. Build in time to relax and acclimatise once you reach your destination, and don't panic if you're not in a state of bliss from day one: it can take several days to unwind enough to start enjoying yourselves.

How Will Being Married Change Things?

Tied up in your ideas about marriage are hopes and dreams that touch on every aspect of your lives. Marriage will affect you in so many ways:

Practical – the kind of home you will have, where you will live, how much money you'll have, your work.

Emotional – love and companionship, friendship, fidelity, the amount of time you'll spend together.

SPEAKING FROM EXPERIENCE

'Our dream was to get married, have our children quickly and after graduation (we were both students) travel to Asia in a minibus. We would educate our children ourselves (in the back of the minibus!) and they, under our expert tuition, would grow up to be well-rounded individuals with a wealth of experience of the world. These dreams were not met, but although I had to work through considerable disappointment, and still daydream about what might have been in my more escapist moments, because the decisions involved were jointly made, they did not have an adverse effect, but rather resulted in a deeper understanding of each other.' BARBIE

Family, including in-laws – they will have lots of expectations about how you'll organise your lives once you're married, including whether you will have children and how you'll care for them.

Marriage will make a difference to many areas of your lives, and provide a backbone of love and stability, but even the most fabulous and fulfilling marriage probably won't answer every single need you've ever had, or ever will have, whether it's for company, for fun and laughter, or for stimulation. Some of your dreams of marriage that you had at the beginning may not be met, but that needn't spell disaster. Together you'll find new dreams to pursue.

Couples who've been together for a while find that, although they might tend to look to each other for comfort and companionship a lot of the time, they also need people and interests outside the marriage as well. That's fine as long as it doesn't threaten your partner or make them feel insecure. The trick lies in keeping the balance between time together and time apart. (See Prioritise Your Relationship, page 135 on how to find the right levels of togetherness for you.)

Second Marriages

If you've already been through a divorce, your expectations of marriage may be complicated by what you've experienced in the past. Ideally, you'll be more realistic about what to expect, and more aware of the problems you might have to face and the best way to deal with them.

It's very common, though, to convince yourself that this time everything will be totally different. The truth is that things can only be different and better if you understand what went wrong before so that you can avoid falling into the same traps again. If you don't know what went wrong and why, you're likely to find some of the same difficulties repeating themselves second time around. It's well worth taking the time to reflect honestly on your previous marriage, painful though that might be, in order to give yourself the best possible chance of happiness this time.

What Will Your Marriage Be Like?

You probably learnt much of what you know about marriage from your family. In the same way that as a child you picked up ways of handling arguments, talking about difficult subjects (or avoiding them) and so on, you also learnt what to expect from a close relationship by observing your parents.

So what? you might say. That was years ago: things are different now and so am I. What has my parents' marriage got to do with mine? Counsellor Gill Bolt says, 'The influence may be

---

SPEAKING FROM EXPERIENCE

'Having been divorced, I find it easy to visualise the kind of situations that could occur between Jade and me when we get married. I know it won't all be plain sailing, because I know the sort of things married couples row about, and how easy it is to get the hump with your wife if she's giving you a hard time. But I also know that Jade won't let anything get to her without talking it out, and that's the big difference. With my first wife, problems would fester for weeks, and nothing ever got sorted out without a blazing row.' DARREN

---

strong or it may be subtle, but it will almost certainly be there. Couples, often without realising it, and even if they have lived together before, can start behaving differently when they are married, acting as if they were their own mother or father. We filter our idea of marriage through the lens of how we experienced our parents' marriage as children, and expectations creep in that have nothing to do with reality.'

If your parents were unmarried or divorced, or you were brought up by a single parent, in a step-parent family, or outside your own family, then your ideas about marriage and the stability of relationships will have been influenced in part by these experiences.

CHECK IT OUT

What have you learnt about marriage in the past?

Check whether you agree or disagree with each statement about your parents' marriage, or, if this is not appropriate, about the most influential adult couple relationship you witnessed in your childhood.

My parents:	Agree	Disagree
• had a good marriage.	☐	☐
• were right to have married each other.	☐	☐
• were good at sorting out problems.	☐	☐
• talked a lot.	☐	☐
• loved each other.	☐	☐
• were faithful to each other.	☐	☐
• would never have contemplated divorce.	☐	☐

- *never bickered.* ☐ ☐
- *believed in marriage.* ☐ ☐
- *were strongly directed by their own families.* ☐ ☐
- *got a lot of support from their own families.* ☐ ☐
- *taught me that marriage was the ideal relationship.* ☐ ☐
- *spent a lot of time together.* ☐ ☐
- *shared everything.* ☐ ☐
- *were seldom apart.* ☐ ☐
- *made independent decisions.* ☐ ☐
- *I'd like my marriage to be like theirs.* ☐ ☐

Reflect on your answers. Do you think they have any bearing on your own ideas about marriage, and if so, is this in a positive or negative way? You'll find other checklists about family influences, in the sections on communication (page 65), handling conflict (page 86) and money (page 111).

Working Out What You Expect

Having thought about why you want to get married, and looked at the kind of family influences that may be at work on your expectations, now think about what your own expectations of marriage really are.

It may be that you can't really imagine what to expect. A lifelong commitment is hard to envisage, and of course, there's no knowing exactly how your lives will develop in future. Even so, it can be useful to focus on the kinds of things you'd like to get from your marriage, to make sure that your hopes are realistic, and likely to be met.

THE BIG QUESTIONS

What do we expect from marriage?

Look at the statements separately, and tick those things that you
are expecting from your marriage. You could cover up your
answers when your partner does the exercise.

Being married will:

- mean that I'll always love and be loved by my
  partner. ☐ ☐
- make me happy. ☐ ☐
- show that our commitment is real. ☐ ☐
- give me a good companion and friend. ☐ ☐
- give me someone I can always talk to about
  everything. ☐ ☐
- mean that I don't need other friends so much. ☐ ☐
- fulfil all my sexual needs. ☐ ☐
- make me feel as if I belong socially. ☐ ☐
- make me feel more grown up. ☐ ☐
- provide a stable home to bring up children. ☐ ☐
- involve total fidelity for both of us. ☐ ☐
- make my family happy. ☐ ☐
- solve a lot of problems. ☐ ☐
- give me financial security. ☐ ☐
- mean making some sacrifices. ☐ ☐
- involve a lot of giving. ☐ ☐
- not always be equal. ☐ ☐
- bring problems over the years. ☐ ☐
- mean that we're always there for each other. ☐ ☐
- mean that we won't fight any more. ☐ ☐

- mean that we'll agree more. ☐ ☐
- mean that my partner will always put me first. ☐ ☐
- make it much harder for us to split up. ☐ ☐

Talk about your findings. Are your expectations very close, or are there noticeable areas of difference? If there are differences, might these cause problems? If either of you feels angry or irritated while you are doing this exercise, don't ignore the feelings but ask yourself what lies behind them. What exactly is it that is making you annoyed? You'll get more out of the exercise by talking about your underlying feelings, even if this does seem difficult.

Loving Across Cultures

With greater freedom to travel and widespread mingling of cultures, many people marry someone who is from a different cultural background.

John O'Reilly, a Relate Clinical Supervisor, has counselled numerous couples in cross-cultural relationships. He says, 'These couples will, of course, have all the usual experiences of adjusting to each other. In a cross-cultural marriage, though, there are other factors to take on board, which can put the relationship under extra pressure.'

John has these tips for success in cross-cultural marriages:
- Find out everything you can about the other's background. Learn about the history of their culture, its family and relationship expectations, religious and spiritual practices, its food, its music – everything.

- Be realistic about your partner's culture. Don't romanticise it and see it as perfect in every respect in comparison to your own culture. Beware, too, of seeing any aspects that you disagree with as meaning that the whole of your partner's culture is bad. All cultures consist of many different elements, some of which you'll feel very comfortable with and others that might make you feel alienated or unsure. Try to see the whole picture rather than focusing on one or two elements.
- Think about and challenge the things you've previously taken for granted about racial differences.
- Step outside the ideas of your own culture when you try to understand those of your partner.
- If your partner is outside the main culture where you live, other people may discriminate against them or be unfriendly or hostile. Your partner will need your understanding and support in coping with this.
- Be sympathetic towards your partner, and imagine what it's like for them to be shifting from one culture into another.
- Don't go along with oppressive beliefs belonging to your partner's culture.
- If you don't have your families' support, or are living far away from them, seek out people who can offer you friendship as a couple.
- Remember, not all your disagreements will be because you are from different backgrounds.
- Keep your own cultural identity alive, and help your partner do the same.
- Develop a joint system of values for yourselves and any children you have.

Predicting the Future

Setting high expectations together means that you have a joint aim in view. Each knowing what the other is hoping for, talking about your dreams for the future and agreeing to focus on keeping your marriage and its well-being as a top priority, puts you in a great position to reach those dreams and enjoy long-lasting fulfilment and stability.

If people go into marriage with unrealistic or unshared expectations, life afterwards becomes much harder. Finding out that marriage isn't going to give them what they hoped for can come as a shattering blow and put the marriage under serious threat.

Don't go down that road. Keep your expectations in mind, and do whatever you can to make sure they are being met. Remember that over the years your needs will alter, and so might some of your expectations. Being married is all about having a shared future, and the future is all about change. Your marriage will be shaped by the way you both adapt and respond to changes.

We're Living Together – Will Getting Married Change Us?

That depends on your view of marriage. Do you think it should or will be different? Look at the reasons you've identified for getting married. Are these different from the reasons you'd give if someone asked you why you were living together?

Suppose, for example, you're getting married because you're expecting your first child, a very common prompt towards formal commitment. Soon after your wedding you'll become a family with a dependent child. Your work patterns will change. There'll be the fun of discovering your new baby – everything will be different. It's not so much the fact of being married that changes things, it's what being married brings with it – in this case, parenthood.

Another reason why things can change when you make the switch from cohabitation to marriage, is that you have hidden expectations about what wives or husbands do or don't do. Are wives such sexy bedmates as live-in lovers? Do husbands go out with the lads as much as live-ins, or know more about putting up shelves? It might sound ridiculous, but many people have a script in their heads about how married people behave, which comes into play when they themselves get married.

Even if you reckon everything will stay much the same, the first year of marriage can have its own glitches. You might:

- feel trapped, or afraid that you've made the wrong choice.
- fantasise about past relationships.
- wonder about how your identity has changed now that you're married.

• agonise about anything that didn't go smoothly at the wedding.

Some couples row more in the first year or so of marriage. You might feel that you've got to sort everything out now because you're in this for life. Irritating habits that used not to bother you so much, might start to bug you.

If this happens to you, don't panic. It takes a while to settle down into a new mode of life, especially if lots of other things are changing simultaneously, as often happens when people get married. For many people, being married is different from living together, even if they didn't expect that it would be. Some find a change occurs in their sex life, while others find that money becomes an issue when it didn't used to be. The chapters on communicating (page 59) and handling disagreements (page 75) can help you, and there are also chapters on specific difficulties such as sex, money or parenting problems (pages 94, 107 and 117), where you'll find more answers.

Looking at Change

Look beyond the wedding day. What kind of things are you expecting to happen in your relationship over the next years? You might be moving abroad, or away from – or closer to – your families. How will this affect you? You might be planning to have children, or have ambitious travel plans. Events like these will have an impact on many areas of your life.

THE BIG QUESTIONS

How do we see our future together?

None of us can know what the future has in store. Even so, thinking about where you would like to be in future is a revealing exercise. Think about these questions in terms of a) next year, b) in five years, c) in ten years.

- Where will we be financially?
- What about children?
- What will we look like?
- How important will sex be?
- Where will we be living?`
- What will be going on in our families?
- What about work, for both of us?
- What other plans do we have?

Doing this exercise can help you see what each other's views and expectations are, and may reveal areas where you have made the wrong assumption about what the other is thinking.

Doubts and Fears

Are you secretly hoping that your partner will change after you're married, or that you will be able to make them different? If so, beware. People change only if they want to, not because other people want them to. If, deep down, you're not sure you could live with aspects of your partner's behaviour, better to face the problem now and get help to try and solve it than to hope that things will be different later on. You need to talk frankly, and if that feels too difficult, counselling might help you.

It's very normal to have the occasional panic before you get married: is this really the right person, am I doing the right thing? If this happens, examine your fears:

- Has something specific triggered them – something your partner does?
- How often have you felt like this?
- What happens to make you feel better about your partner again?
- Are your feelings about your partner more positive or negative? It can help to jot down a list and see where the balance lies.
- Do you ever compare life with your partner to your life in past relationships?
- If so, how does it measure up?
- Are you happy to go ahead with your wedding?

Postponing or cancelling the wedding

If your doubts are so serious that you're not sure you want to go through with your wedding, be brave. It's vital that you take responsibility for your own future happiness. Putting the brakes on will be messy, hurtful and sad, but how much worse will it be if you go through with a marriage that, in your heart, you know to be wrong for you?

- If you can, go to counselling with your partner so that you can understand together why the relationship isn't working out.
- If you're feeling scared, but are not completely sure that you want to back out, put the wedding plans on hold temporarily. Remove the pressure and give yourself as much space and time as you need to decide whether this marriage is right for you or not.
- If you decide not to go ahead, you must be brave and bring the relationship to an end. Although you will feel that you are letting a lot of people down, you will do far more harm if you go ahead knowing that the marriage has little chance of succeeding.
- The money that has already been spent prior to the wedding often stops people calling a halt. But think how much worse it will be if you and your families spend thousands of pounds on the wedding day, reception and honeymoon, only to face the misery of the marriage falling to pieces a year down the line.

The Relate Couples Course

Time spent thinking about what you hope for from each other, where the conflicts lie, and how best to resolve them is time well invested. Relationships need thought and action in order to flourish, and if things aren't perfect, it's often possible to make changes for the better.

The Relate Couples Course (see page 9 for details) offers an opportunity to learn more about yourselves and your relationship.

Couples who go on this course learn about a whole range of very effective skills that they can easily use to make their relationship even better and more satisfying.

Going on a course to prepare for marriage is a great start to the rest of your lives together. This is the time when many elements of your relationship might need deeper understanding or renegotiating, and couples who've been on the courses have found them very rewarding and thought-provoking, as well as good fun. Meeting other couples who are at the same stage in their lives can

---

SPEAKING FROM EXPERIENCE

Comments from couples who have been on a Relate Couples Course

'The day was really helpful. It's such a good idea and gave us an excellent grounding for married life together.'

'I felt very at ease on the course, the approach was open and friendly.'

'It was so helpful hearing what other people had to say, and made me realise that others are experiencing the same joys/difficulties as we are.'

'I realise now that Relate's not all to do with confronting huge problems. Even in a strong relationship, learning ways to solve the small problems so that they never get to be huge can make a difference.'

'I thought I knew it all, but the course has shown me lots of things I hadn't thought about properly before.'

'Stimulating and thought-provoking, and I could see the links to the way we live our lives.'

'Definitely worthwhile, and I still want to marry him!'

> *'When you get married, kindly old people tell you that marriage has to be worked on. Sadly, no one ever tells you what this work is, or whether you can get a man in to do it for you.'* GUY BROWNING

also help to reassure you that everyone feels a whole mix of emotions before they get married. It's totally normal to be excited, but equally normal to feel a little scared.

The Relate Couples Course focuses on showing people different ways of communicating, and helping them to reflect on their relationships and the way they want them to be. Using these straightforward techniques in your day-to-day lives when you're married can go a long way towards preventing problems in the future.

Summary

- Share your marriage wish-list with each other.
- Think big and set high expectations.
- Reflect on the reasons why you are getting married.
- Be prepared for changes in the early days and in the future.
- Face up to doubts and fears – they're normal.
- Learn how to get the very best out of your marriage.

2

Make a Lasting Commitment

Making a lifetime's commitment to each other is the root from which a fulfilling and enriching relationship can spring. Saying the words out loud during the wedding ceremony is just the start. Real commitment shows through in the way you behave towards each other day after day, year after year. It's something you can constantly build on to enhance and deepen your relationship as time goes by.

Marriage is exciting, and full of marvellous possibilities. This is your chance to build the future you want together. There's no simple prescription. Each marriage is unique, as unique as the man and woman involved, and it's only by living your marriage together that you'll discover the vital ingredients that make it work for you. The key is for both partners to put a lot into the relationship and never take it for granted. To live with someone else for years, to see each other through thick and thin, to create a shared history and a shared life takes energy, involvement and caring. It isn't always easy but by doing it you can create an enriching and sustaining relationship that will underpin your lives with a sense of love, acceptance and stability.

THE BIG QUESTIONS

What does commitment mean?

It's important to the lasting strength of your relationship that the idea of commitment means much the same to both of you. Look through this list of things that making a lifelong commitment might involve, and see how important you think each one is.

- Loving each other enough to be able to withstand problems and upsets.
- Being faithful.
- Never telling lies.
- Trusting each other.
- Working out a balance we are both happy with between the amount of time we give to our own relationship and the amount we give to outside interests, our children, families and friends, and other commitments.
- Working at reaching agreements on the things that are important to us.
- Trying to keep other potentially difficult relationships, such as those with an ex-spouse, at a level that doesn't threaten our relationship.
- Making time specially for us.

How do you feel about each of these? Some of them may be hard to achieve, especially if you have children from a previous relationship to consider. Maybe there are other important things that you want to add. Talk about what you have discovered.

Getting married gives you a shared interest in the lastingness of your relationship. You've decided to give it your all, whatever that involves. Sustaining a commitment calls for a lot of giving, a lot of compromising, and there'll be times when you'll have to put your partner's needs before your own.

THE BIG QUESTIONS

Whose needs come first?

Most couples sort out the daily give and take when they live together, and get used to considering each other's wants and needs. Maybe you can't lie in the bath uninterrupted for two hours, or watch your favourite TV programmes every day, but making little compromises over this kind of thing isn't such a big deal. The really major sacrifices, though, the ones you need to make in those times when life hurls a bucketful of icy water in your face, those can test your commitment to the limits. Read what happened to the following couples, and reflect on how both of you might respond in a similar situation.

- **Leaving family and friends behind**

  Amy and John met and married in London. Then his job moved to Scotland, so they had to uproot and start again, hundreds of miles from the place where they felt most at home.

- **Mother-in-law moving in**

  Samir and Julie married in the UK, where his family, who were originally from Egypt, also lived. When Samir's father died, Samir assumed that his mother would move in with them because he felt it was his duty to take care of her.

- **One partner's serious illness**

  Lynn and Phil had been married for 18 months and were expecting their first child when Phil was involved in a car crash which left him with serious spinal injuries.

- **An unexpected family**

  When Steve's ex-wife became ill, his two children suddenly had to move in with Steve and his new wife, Magda.

How would you handle a testing situation? Sometimes there simply isn't a compromise, and someone has to give way. Remember, though, that even potentially devastating experiences can also have the power to enrich and reinforce a relationship. Everything depends on how the two partners respond. How well would your relationship stand up to a real test?

Keeping a Sense of Self

A study carried out by the University of Nottingham discovered that younger married couples striving to invest in both their relationship and their own personal development found it 'extremely difficult' to achieve a balance. As individuals, you each have an independent identity. As a couple, you develop a third identity, something different and bigger, that involves both of you putting aside some of your desire for total independence and allowing yourselves to become interdependent. This can feel very risky, and often causes real upsets in the early stages of a relationship. For a marriage to work well, both partners need to accept and enjoy their interdependency without losing sight of their individual identities to the extent that they feel consumed by coupledom.

Getting that balance between keeping enough freedom and sense of self, while at the same time taking your partner's needs and wants into account, demands flexibility and understanding on both sides.

A Lifetime Together

Not so long ago, marrying for life meant spending 20 or 30 years together if you were lucky. Today, with life expectancies of 80 years or more, the average couple who wed when they're around 30 could be looking forward to 50 years of marriage.

Believing wholeheartedly that this relationship is the one you want to be in 50 years down the line is a great kick-off point. Research shows that relationships fare better when couples sense that theirs is a strong bond that will last into the foreseeable future. Promising to be there for each other come what may for the

'It's a sobering thought that almost two-thirds of marriages in this country end happily.' GUY BROWNING

rest of your lives is a big promise to make, but not so outrageous.
Although it is sad but true that many marriages end in divorce, it
is equally true that an even greater number last, and last into the
long-term future. A satisfying and lasting marriage is a reality for
many people.

Face the Future Together

The public commitment you make on your wedding day is just the
beginning. Over the years that bond will change. In a good
marriage, it will become deeper and more profound.

Couples who've been together for many years have had their
commitment to each other tested, often many times. The outcome

frequently depends on what is happening in their relationships because commitment isn't static. If your partner abuses your trust, for instance, your commitment will be shaken and may even be destroyed. Making the initial commitment of marrying, on the other hand, can give you the resolve you need later on to overcome problems that might otherwise have put your relationship on the skids.

CHECK IT OUT

Test your commitment

Look at these statements and consider how true each one is for you. Get your partner to do the same.

- This relationship feels very right, and I am in it because that's where I want to be.
- I feel very positive and excited about our future life together.
- I know staying married will take effort and compromise and I'm willing to do that.
- My partner and I think of ourselves as a couple with dreams and goals in common.
- I'm not interested in the idea of starting a new relationship with anyone else.
- We have discussed and are agreed on whether or not we want children, and when we would like to have them.
- I expect to grow old with my partner and to share the rest of our lives.

Think carefully about what each of these statements means, and talk them over together.

SPEAKING FROM EXPERIENCE

'My wife is Gujarati, and by marrying her I also took on a seriously extended family. Asian families do lots of visiting with each other – they love it. Sometimes I'd be with her at her mum and dad's house, and they'd all be speaking Gujarati – not intending to exclude me, but just doing it without thinking – and I'd be stuck in a corner thinking, 'When can I escape?' I'd get so miserable that sometimes I'd just leg it. We've had to do a lot of digging, a lot of understanding, work harder than couples who come from the same background, to work out a compromise between her family's closeness and my need for privacy.' PHIL, MARRIED TO JYOTI FOR 17 YEARS

Commitment feeds on prosaic, practical factors. For it to last, both partners must be fundamentally happy and satisfied with each other, and want to stick together. The marriage is even more firmly cemented if you've both made big investments – possibly financial, and definitely emotional – in the relationship, which would turn into major losses if you left. This, for instance, could include putting joint time and effort into raising children, or creating a home together.

Undoubtedly, there will be times ahead when your marriage will come under serious strain, and one or other, or even both of you, might weigh up the pros and cons of staying or quitting. The more chance your commitment has had to grow before it comes under pressure, the more likely it is to be strong enough to ride the rough times.

How can we build on our commitment to each other?

Counsellors and other marriage experts offer these thoughts on how to build a strong foundation to your marriage.

- Think to the future and about where you both want to be in five or ten years. If you have been married before, think honestly about what went wrong.
- Be prepared to be the first to change your behaviour, and the first to apologise.
- Be alive to your marriage, and if things are going wrong, do something about it sooner rather than later.
- Bite your lip and keep any nasty thoughts about your partner to yourself.
- Set high standards for the relationship. Don't tolerate bad behaviour early on in the hopes that things will get better – they won't.
- Find something about your marriage to enjoy every day.
- Solve arguments and leave them behind. Don't sulk or let them fester.
- Give lots of strokes and positive contact.
- Learn to express your thoughts without your partner feeling offended or having to defend themselves.
- Listen.
- Be sure that your expectations are attainable.
- Understand that your partner can't be everything. You both need other people in your life.

'I had to leave everyone behind'

The biggest test for John and Amy was when, out of the blue, John accepted a job in Aberdeen. Amy had no wish to leave London, where she'd always lived, and where all her friends and family were. If it had been just the two of them, the move would have been the end of the road: much as Amy loved John, she wouldn't have gone. 'But we've two children to consider and I couldn't bear the hurt we'd cause by splitting up, so I went with him. That was so, so hard.'

Counsellors say: *'If you give up something important, the hurt and loss to you should be recognised and valued. Your partner should try to compensate you in some way so that you don't feel completely powerless.'*

Making a Commitment, Second Time Around

What is the secret of making a second marriage work? People who achieve a happy new relationship may feel regret and sorrow at the ending of their previous marriage, but at the same time they have seized the opportunity to learn from the experience. Having faced the failure and the reasons for it, they've discovered that it is possible to go forward better equipped to deal with the conflicts of life as half a couple, and also readier to appreciate the pleasures.

If it's your second time around, grab the chance to practise consciously, compromise and communication, skills that may have been lacking before. Begin to understand the real meaning of a commitment, what it demands and the rewards it brings. In letting the past influence the present positively, you can even use a new marriage to work out old, unresolved problems in a different, safer setting.

REAL LIVES

Scared of marrying a second time

Adam and Maggie were both divorced when they met. Both of them were very wary about remarrying because the experience of divorce had been so painful. They took their relationship one cautious step at a time, both keeping their own flats to begin with, but staying over with each other several nights a week. After a couple of years they bought a house together. A year later, they decided to have a child. Only when Maggie was pregnant, did they agree to marry. 'It may seem illogical, but the house and baby were huge commitments: once we'd made those, it seemed the obvious thing to get married. We'd gradually come to trust each other enough to see ourselves as a unit, going on into the future, and that made remarrying possible, whereas before it had been too risky.'

Counsellors say: 'It can feel dangerous to perceive yourself as a unit because you might split up and be hurt, or lose your sense of self. But it's only by doing so that you can really start to believe in your marriage and put the best of yourself into it without holding anything back.'

Understanding and accepting yourself and your partner, building a firm foundation of love and making a real commitment are the ingredients that a second marriage needs. They are none of them easy, but they are all valuable. The day will never arrive when you can say, 'This is exactly the way this relationship should be, and from now on it will be like this all the time.' Success is much more

---

SPEAKING FROM EXPERIENCE

On Second Marriages

'Exercise rational caution, but don't give up hope of success despite a first failure. Equally, don't be too starry-eyed. Talk about issues before they become issues. Demonstrate your love for the other person: saying "I love you" or giving tiny spontaneous presents keeps a sense of warmth and vitality.' PHILIP

'Don't be in a rush to marry. Wait. Be brave and spend some time trying to cope alone if you can. Live together first. Ask yourself why you want to marry again. If it's for financial reasons, or for company, you're on a sticky road. Marriage requires care, understanding, trust and freedom.' LAURA

'Our relationship began as an affair at work, and although he did leave his wife for me and we did marry, the marriage lasted only 18 months. I would say to anyone, think very carefully before you break up a tried and tested relationship. A relationship that starts in disloyalty and involves the breaking of ties often repeats that pattern. Men in particular often miss the comfort of home, the acceptance of family.' BECKY

---

elusive and fragmented. You might get it right one day and wrong the next, or have a good phase lasting weeks followed by a storm. Never mind. Learning to live together means learning to accept and trust; it means forgiving yourself and your partner when either of you gets it wrong; and it means trying that bit harder to get it right. See it as a joint, lifelong enterprise and an opportunity for permanent and enriching change, and you're halfway there. Couples can and do succeed together when both have failed before.

From Cohabitation To Marriage

Around 70 per cent of couples live together before they get married. Although patterns are changing, at the moment, two-thirds of young couples marry within ten years of moving in together.

Some cohabiting couples choose never to marry, of course, perhaps because for them the institution seems intrusive or irrelevant, or because they want to keep their legal independence. Couples who have been married before and been through the trauma of divorce may be reluctant to enshrine any new relationship within the law. The commitment between these couples may be just as strong as that between married couples.

For many others, there is a definite difference between living together and marrying. When people marry because marriage itself has a real meaning for them and is something that they both want to do, their commitment is likely to become deeper than it was when they were cohabiting. At what point they decide to marry doesn't matter. Many have already made numerous binding commitments to each other, such as having children or buying a joint house. What is important is that both partners want marriage for the same reasons, and have similar expectations of what marriage will bring.

'Only one of us wanted to marry'

Greg and Tasha had lived together for six years, and had a three-year-old daughter. Marriage was never on the agenda, but suddenly Tasha said she wanted to get married. Greg had always gone along with what she wanted, but he felt pressurised and said no. The more he dug his heels in, the more Tasha wanted to marry him. In her mind, getting married would prove that he loved her and make her feel secure.

Counsellors say: 'People who have lived together for many years and then decide to marry sometimes do it because there is something wrong in the relationship, although they may not be aware of it. But marriage doesn't solve problems. Ask yourself, "What am I hoping for from marriage?" Give the other person a chance to think without pressure. It's very hard, but the decision to marry should always be arrived at together.'

Arranged Marriages

In arranged marriages, couples are introduced via family members, but have the freedom to decide whether or not they want to marry.

The marriage of Harish Patel, a lecturer in architecture, and Urvashi, a social worker, was arranged 25 years ago. 'People in this country often misunderstand how the system of arranging marriages works,' he says. 'They say, "Had you met before the wedding day?" and I tell them, "Of course – we knew each other well." '

Harish and Urvashi were introduced by a friend of the family. 'I was 23 and thinking seriously about getting married,' says Harish. 'Our friend asked what kind of person I had in mind, and I said that I was interested not in a beautiful face, but in a beautiful personality. He then talked separately to Urvashi, who wanted a husband who was highly educated, tall and of a similar age to herself.' With the agreement of both families, the couple were introduced. 'We knew each other for six months, and spent a lot of time together before we decided to become betrothed,' says Harish. 'We weren't strangers at all, although there was no physical intimacy between us before marriage. But otherwise we were inseparable.

'What we wanted was a 50/50 partnership for a lifetime, and that is what we have. Really, having an arranged marriage like ours is rather like looking for a partner through a dating agency, except it is more strictly controlled by the families. A dating agency would put the details into a computer, whereas for us our friend assessed our compatibility, found out about our likes and dislikes, and dovetailed the arrangements.'

THE BIG QUESTIONS

Why do I sometimes feel scared that my marriage won't work out?

It's normal to have some anxieties before you get married – everyone does. Face your fears, together if possible. Don't risk ignoring them.

- Consider the big questions such as 'What will happen if we have children?' before the wedding. Don't think 'We'll sort that out when we're married'. Feelings about big issues tend to emerge gradually, over a long period of time, so find out what your partner is thinking now.

- If something is worrying you – maybe your partner is reluctant to talk about your future, or sometimes behaves in a way that you find totally unacceptable – check things out with someone who isn't closely involved, not your friends or parents. You can go to Relate on your own for help. One or two sessions with an impartial counsellor could be enough to help you work out what's best to do.
- Look at your fears and try to understand them. Once a problem or worry is out in the open, it often loses its scariness.

Occasional misgivings are very understandable in the run-up to taking such an important step as marriage. See also page 36 for more about understanding the significance of your doubts and fears.

When Does a Problem Become a Serious Threat?

In the days when divorce was virtually impossible, many people were stuck in miserable marriages because getting out wasn't an option. Now divorce, unpalatable as it might be, is something that many couples would consider if their marriage ran into serious difficulties. Although the actual number of divorces (141,135) in the year 2000 was the lowest for over 20 years, there's nothing to be complacent about in the fact that 40 per cent of marriages end in court. That figure means that of the 268,000 couples who took their vows in 2000, about 107,000 will eventually divorce. This represents a huge cost, both in terms of the misery experienced by thousands of couples and children, and the estimated £5 billion expense borne by the State.

The trouble is, once it becomes possible to escape from a marriage, it also becomes harder to decide whether a problem is terminal or can somehow be resolved, given enough joint time and will. Throughout this book, you'll find suggestions to help you anticipate and troubleshoot problems before they turn into real threats to your future together. You'll also find techniques for communicating better and handling conflicts productively.

THE BIG QUESTIONS

Can we divorce-proof our marriage?

Sometimes, divorces are precipitated by events that are outside the couple's control. It isn't possible to protect yourselves against everything that might happen in your lives. That said, there are elements you can encourage into your relationship that can strengthen it and help it withstand the testing times.

Your prospects of a lasting and happy marriage are good if you:

- Have realistic expectations of what marriage will be like.
- Have begun to work out good ways of communication.
- Can often sort out rows and disagreements so that both are satisfied with the outcome.

- Have some leisure interests in common.
- Are both happy with your sex life.
- Know each other well and are not rushing into marriage impetuously.
- Agree on how much time you will spend with family and friends, both together and separately.
- Have worked out who does what within your day-to-day relationship, so that both feel OK with the roles they play.
- Foster these elements in your relationship: friendship, love, loyalty/trust, honesty, humour, freedom/independence, tenderness, respect, a bit of unpredictability, compatibility, shared interests.

Does the list alert you to any areas where you could usefully talk and think about your relationship together? Look through other sections of this book for more detail on many of these topics.

Change, Change and Change Again

A wedding is just the beginning. A declaration, a celebration, a statement of mutual intent, the start of a new level of commitment – it's all of these. Marriage, though, is different: an unpredictable

SPEAKING FROM EXPERIENCE

'Establishing that your commitment has no let-out clause and that parting is not an option creates a secure foundation for working through even the most sensitive and painful issues. Learning to forgive and be forgiven on a regular basis prevents the relationship going sour.'
BARBIE, MARRIED FOR 32 YEARS TO PETER

journey of change, unique to every couple, that will lead them through who-knows-what uncharted waters. A marriage is made of shared experience, enriched by mutual enjoyments and strengthened by tribulations weathered. To succeed, it must respond to all the changes that will undoubtedly take place in your lives.

'Working at a marriage' may sound like a lot of effort for something that's supposed to be fun, but there's no doubt that if you put nothing in, you'll get precious little out. Marriage needs time and energy from both partners, plus a willingness to tackle problems as and when they arise. Keep your relationship central, no matter how busy you are down the years with careers, children and the rest, and be prepared to change and change again as life alters you both. That way you'll build the bedrock of a marriage that enriches and enhances both your lives for ever.

Summary

- Making a lifetime's commitment is creative and exciting.
- You won't always be able to put your own needs first.
- Learn to build on your relationship so that it can tolerate strains.
- Success is possible second time around.
- Put a lot into your marriage and you'll get a lot out.

3

Keep Talking

One of the best things about being married is that there's always someone who's on your side. If you have a problem, there's someone you can talk it over with, who knows you inside out and understands just what makes you tick. If you're feeling down, your partner knows just what to say to make you smile.

Being able to communicate well is often held up as the vital element in successful relationships. But what exactly *is* good communication? For most people, getting their message across is a hit and miss business. How well it happens depends on who you are talking to, how tired you are, what else is happening, and how much you care about what's being said. Communication tactics that work like a charm for one couple won't cut any ice with another: the way people prefer to connect with each other is a very individual thing.

Communicating well might mean doing lots of talking, but body language is also a good indicator of how your partner's feeling. A smile, a passing caress, a wink, a touch, a contented sigh all give off vibes, and as you become more and more tuned in to each other, you'll start to know what kind of day your partner's had, just by the way they walk in through the door.

Listening Matters

Lengthy, in-depth conversations suit some couples, while others prefer to use fewer words and let their actions do some of the talking. It's important to work out ways of communicating that suit *you* so that you can:

- develop insight and understanding about each other.
- learn to predict how the other might respond to things that happen or are said.
- express love and show appreciation.
- sort out problems.
- keep track of each other's concerns.

These are all things that strengthen a marriage, and help the relationship to keep pace as partners change.

Not that it's just about talking. Listening – and most importantly, really hearing – is the other side of the equation. To be listened to properly and feel understood is the key to communicating well, and all it takes is a bit of time and concentration.

THE BIG QUESTIONS

What's stopping you from hearing?

Many things get in the way when two people are trying to talk something out. Say, for instance, that the topic under discussion is going on holiday. Both partners start from their own frame of reference, and these could be very different. Beaches, sun, and total chill-out might be what holidays are all about for her. Put him on a beach for more than an hour, though, and he ends up bad-tempered and bored. There's no way he wants to go anywhere that doesn't have a good range of sports activities on offer.

It's very easy to assume that your partner feels the same way that you do about any given subject. But to talk constructively, both people must first make sure that they know where the other is coming from.

There's zero chance of being heard if she starts the conversation when he's listening to the football results, or he launches off when she's deep in her book. Talk that has to fight with distractions is, for the listener, like a crackle on the radio – irritating at best, and at worst, enough to make them switch off.

Next time you've got something to discuss:

- Pick a time when there are no distractions. Turn the TV off, or agree on a suitable time.
- Make eye contact with the speaker and show that you are listening by nodding, paying attention, encouraging them to carry on, saying 'yes', or 'uh uh' to show you are still listening.
- When they've finished, repeat back some of what was said: 'So you'd be happy as long as there are things for you to do while I'm sunbathing.' This shows that you've taken their message on board.
- Even if you disagree, give the other's opinion your time and consideration. Be willing to shift your own position in order to reach a happy compromise.

Poor communication means that someone ends up feeling misunderstood, unheard and resentful. There may be a row or a silence. Either way, nothing gets sorted. Good communication means that both of you have had a chance to say what you want and be heard. You've understood each other's point of view, and done your best to reach a compromise that makes you both happy.

'He's so different now.'

Janette and Bill had been married for two years. Janette complained that lately Bill didn't seem to want to talk to her at all, and would never offer an opinion on anything. 'When I first knew him he was very outgoing, but after we were married he changed. I suppose he stopped trying to impress me. I wanted this confident man, but what I got was someone who never disagreed and was too easy to please.' In counselling, Janette realised that Bill had stopped talking to her because he was afraid of her anger – nothing he did was right. Janette needed to think about her anger – what was at the root of it, and how could she express it so that it wasn't destructive. She began to understand that she could still love him as the man he really was, but that she would have to alter her approach to the way they communicated, and stop expecting Bill to be something that he wasn't. Bill also needed to think about why he wasn't more assertive.

Counsellors say: *'If someone says, "You're not the person I married", it needn't mean that the relationship will end. It's possible to adapt to changes in other people. Communication involves understanding how and why your partner takes a different approach from you and leaving room for compromise. Throughout your marriage there will be changes. Nothing and nobody stays exactly the same, so talking about the changes and how they make you feel is very important.'*

CHECK IT OUT

What do you know about listening and talking?

Susan Quilliam, in her book *The Relate Guide to Staying Together* (see page 199), says that everyone has times when they don't communicate as well as they'd like to. She suggests that to understand more about the way you communicate, you complete the following sentences:

- I remember being afraid to talk because...
- I remember saying something I regretted when...
- A time something I said made a real difference was when...
- A time when I misheard something and it caused trouble was when...
- A time I listened to someone and really helped was when...

Thinking about good and less good experiences that you've had can help you to identify better ways of communicating. Don't lash yourself when things go wrong, but instead take the opportunity to think about how you could do it better next time.

In a survey carried out by BT Forum 95 per cent of the people questioned thought that failing marriages could be saved if couples were able to talk to each other. Despite this, a quarter admitted that they never talked about their relationship with their partner.

Learning to Listen

In the early months and years of a relationship, most couples can't hear enough of what the other has to say, and lie awake half the night talking and talking. As time goes by, and the demands of day-to-day life and perhaps a family, impinge on the romance, you settle into a comfortableness with each other where meaningful talk doesn't happen so much. There's no time, or you've forgotten how.

It's easy to get out of the habit of talking about important things and into the way of discussing only the more trivial aspects of your lives, like what's on TV, office gossip. It can be hard to broach more testing subjects, but the more often you do it, the easier it will become.

Improve the way you listen

Many couples who go to Relate put their problems down to a lack – sometimes a total lack – of communication. After all, if you don't talk about your problems, how can you attempt to solve them? If you think you're not communicating too well, try this approach to learning to listen, which many people have used very successfully. It need take only about 15 minutes. Agree on a time that suits you both, when you won't be disturbed and both feel alert and ready to have a go at really talking.

One of you has five minutes to speak while the other listens. The speaker should stay off the subject of the relationship to start with, and talk about something straightforward that has happened to them lately, and how they felt about it. The other has to concentrate on listening well, quietly paying attention and taking a real interest in what is being said. That's it. When the speaker has finished, there's no need to discuss what was said.

Swap over, and have another five minutes of speaking/listening.

If you can do this a couple of times a week, you'll find that you gradually become much better listeners. As that happens, you can give the speaker more time to talk, repeat back what was said to check understanding, and move on to more difficult subjects.

CHECK IT OUT

What did you learn from your family about communication?

Children pick up all sorts of messages about talking and listening from their families, some of which they go on to use as adults. Recognising the patterns of communication, both helpful and less constructive, that your family used, can be a big step towards understanding how you can change or improve the ways you communicate now. Think about these questions:

- Who made the decisions in your family?
- Were decisions affecting the whole family discussed with the children?
- What happened when your parents disagreed?
- Was it acceptable to show anger? Who was allowed to show anger and who wasn't? What happened when someone was angry?
- Did your parents laugh together and seem to enjoy each other's company?
- Did people talk about their feelings or just show them by their behaviour?
- If there was a lot of talking, how constructive was it in solving problems?

- Did people listen properly to each other and try to understand, or did they make assumptions about how other family members were feeling?

Answer the questions, then think about your responses. How have these experiences shaped the way you communicate today? Is there anything you'd like to change? Share what you find with your partner, and ask them to answer the questions as well.

Showing That You Care

There are more ways to showing your feelings for your partner than saying 'I love you' – words that, for some people, do not trip easily off the tongue. Most people have favourite ways of

---

SPEAKING FROM EXPERIENCE

'Looking back, I can see that my father got what he wanted by shouting the rest of us down. We were afraid to argue with him because when he lost his temper he would storm about slamming doors, or if we were in the car, he would put his foot down and drive like a maniac until he'd calmed down. So it was safer to do things his way. For years I've followed his example and tried to get my own way by shouting, swearing or kicking the furniture. Relationships have bust up over my rages. My fiancée, Angie, is different, though. She won't tolerate it, and when I start she says that classic thing, "You sound just like your dad". It pulls me up short: I don't want to go down that road and have everyone scared of me.' STEPHEN, 34

---

expressing and receiving love. Which of the approaches listed here might appeal to your partner? Which would you most like to receive? In the early years together, you'll probably do some of these things automatically and frequently, and it's important not to let these habits lapse as time goes by.

Positive talk
- Be kind, offer encouragement.
- Ask, rather than demand.
- Say how much you appreciate what your partner does for you.

Positive actions
- Do the chores you know your partner would like you to do without being nagged.
- Don't treat your spouse like a servant.
- Give gifts without waiting for a special occasion. You don't have to spend a fortune, but make it something that shows you've thought about what your partner would like.
- Give of yourself, your time, your attention. When there's a clash of interests, don't always give your other interests priority – put your partner first.
- Have proper conversations about things that interest you both and are important.

Touch

- Hold hands, kiss, hug, give a massage.
- Touch often – don't save all your caresses for the times when you have, or want to have, sex.
- Kiss on parting and re-meeting – not a cursory peck, but a kiss with some feeling behind it.

THE BIG QUESTIONS

How can we communicate better?

Think about these pointers towards communicating well, and reflect on how much you use them already, and which ones you think could be useful to try.

- Say what you really mean, with no hedging.
- Admit when something is annoying you, rather than pretending that everything's OK.
- Stick to the topic you want to talk about without wandering off at a tangent.
- Don't take refuge in silence. Nothing can be resolved unless you talk about it.
- Respond like an adult. Don't play the child with, 'It's not fair', or lay down the law in heavy-parent mode.
- Never assume that you know what your partner is going to say before they've said it.
- Let your partner make their point without interrupting.
- Avoid holding forth on how you feel about something. Let your partner have a say, too.
- Stay with the subject, even when it's difficult, until you're both ready to stop.

- Take responsibility for your own feelings.
- Listen to what is being said when someone is criticising you, and ask yourself whether or not what they are saying is reasonable.

Communicating well takes practice and a willingness to air difficult or sensitive topics when necessary, rather than letting them fester. Once you recognise the best ways to communicate, you can start to be more open and receptive with each other. Over time you'll find that you have fewer disagreements, and become much better at nipping problems in the bud by talking about them.

It's in Your Voice

How you say what you say affects the way you are heard. Shouting and swearing, being dismissive, patronising or abrupt won't endear you to your partner, and will make him or her far less likely to listen. If your partner treats you in any of these ways, what can you do?

- Refuse to continue the conversation unless you are treated politely and with respect.
- Say, 'I won't carry on talking to you while you are using that tone of voice.'
- Leave the room until your partner calms down. Explain why you are leaving.
- When things have calmed down, say how you felt when your partner used this unpleasant behaviour. Did it make you feel undervalued or frightened, for instance?
- Tell your partner that it is their behaviour you don't like, not them as a person.

When to Keep a Secret

Most of us have one or two no-go areas, events in the past that we would prefer to forget, and certainly don't want to talk about. There might be many areas of life where one person has something they haven't shared with their partner, such as a bad experience in a past relationship, being fired, terminating a pregnancy, or causing a serious family rift.

If you fear that telling your secret would hurt your partner and damage your relationship, stop and think. Although marriage does involve a high level of trust built on openness and honesty, you also have a right to privacy about your past, especially if the secret is not relevant to your current relationship.

If you do decide to tell your secret, and are anxious about the best way to do it, try talking the whole matter over with a trusted friend beforehand. This can help you to get your anxieties into proportion, as well as giving you a chance to rehearse what you want to say. When you do tell your partner, give them a chance to think about what you've said for a while before you discuss it any further.

Create a Positive Emphasis

Every day partners communicate with each other dozens of times, from asking when the shower will be free to suggesting that it's time for bed. On each and every occasion you can make choices about the words you use, your tone of voice, whether you're nice to your partner or whether you give them a hard time.

All those little exchanges in themselves might seem trivial, but they really count. In time, they add up to an overall atmosphere of affection or antagonism within a marriage that has a colossal impact on its long-term prospects. When leading American marriage guru John Gottman investigated which marriages are most likely to fail, he discovered that, for success, a couple need to give each other five times as many positives every day as negatives. Each nag, snappy remark or failure to listen is a minus. Every smile, touch, shared laugh or pleasant exchange is a positive. Even if you have occasional blazing rows in between times, if the underlying 'mood' of your marriage is positive, it has an excellent chance of lasting long term.

It's very easy to slip into the habit of taking your partner for granted, half-listening, and seldom giving them the positive responses that can make them feel so much better. The following simple techniques can help put the accent on the positive.

- Stop what you're doing when your partner wants to talk, and listen.
- Show affection by sitting close to each other, holding hands when walking etc.
- Call or text your partner with caring messages.
- Pay your partner compliments: show that you are proud of them.
- Enjoy being silly together and sharing private jokes.
- Take a real interest in each other's lives. Listen when your partner wants to tell you about their day.

Asking for Change

There will be times when you want to ask your partner to alter the way they behave, or when you are planning a change and want their agreement.

Not only do most people have an in-built resistance to change, but many interpret any request to be different as criticism, and therefore give it the thumbs down.

- If you want your partner to alter their behaviour, try phrasing your complaint like this: 'When you... I feel...'. For example, 'When you don't listen, it makes me feel that you don't care.' This is more effective than going in with a direct criticism – 'You never listen to a word I say' – which puts the other person on the defensive and leaves the way open for a row.
- Don't get into a slanging match by being rude about your partner or teasing them unkindly.
- If your partner comes back at you angrily or hurtfully, don't respond in the same way. Stay calm and say something pleasant – this makes it harder for a row to develop.

- Make a specific request for the change you would like rather than being vague: 'Please can you put the cereal back in the cupboard and your bowl in the dishwasher,' rather than, 'The kitchen's a total tip, as usual.'
- Beware of assuming that you know what your partner thinks about the issue you are raising.
- Don't make threats, either physical or emotional.

CHECK IT OUT

It winds me up

Most people have habits that irritate their partners, often without realising. It's not always possible to wipe these out completely, but you can try by asking how your partner could work on their habit, and what you could do to help them. For example:

Problem: It gets on my nerves when my girlfriend bites her nails.

She could: Try to reduce the stress in her life because she bites her nails most when she's under pressure.

I could: With her agreement, remind her gently to stop each time she starts – often she doesn't realise she's doing it.

'A discussion that starts, "I'll tell you something you do that irritates me, if you tell me something I do that bothers you," never ends in a hug and kiss.' PHYLLIS DILLER, COMEDIENNE

Take Your Time

Once you've hit on ways of communicating that work for you, use them whenever you have something to say to each other. Consciously work at keeping positive 'strokes' going in your relationship, something that often falls by the wayside when you've been together for a year or two. Bit by bit, tackle the areas where you know that the way you communicate leaves something to be desired, and improve things. Doing this will pay dividends every time you run into a problem or conflict of interests.

Summary

- Hone your listening skills so that your partner always feels heard.
- Discover surefire ways to show how much you care.
- Use simple and effective techniques to get useful talk flowing.
- Make small, loving gestures every day to put your marriage on track for long-term success.
- Learn how to ask for change – and get it.

4

Resolve Conflict

Marriage is a package deal. You get your partner, with all their funny habits and foibles, you get their history, their family – and you get your very own collection of rows. Researchers who have followed up married couples find that five years on, couples are still rowing about the same things they fought over as newly-weds.

Sounds dreadful, but does it matter? All couples argue from time to time: that's life. And because people seldom change fundamentally (remember that), the niggles that cause upsets early on, such as spending habits, untidiness or lateness, are still likely to be issues ten years later.

The crux is not the fact that you have rows – even a lot of rows – but how you handle those rows, and how they affect your relationship. Couples who learn to accept their differences and view them with affection and humour fare far better than those who become entrenched in exasperation and bitterness.

'I love being married. It's so great to find one special person you want to annoy for the rest of your life.' RITA RUDNER, COMEDIENNE

> *'We're both really mouthy and volatile. Sometimes we can have a big row and make up five times a day if we're bored.'* MAXINE

How do You Row?

For some couples, regular heated quarrels are the norm. Once they've had a good shouting match, they can go on to resolve their differences. Others hate any type of conflict, and will go out of their way to avoid it. Then there are couples who enjoy talking through their problems, and get them sorted that way.

None of these approaches is any better or worse than another. Couples are different, and exactly how they handle conflicts doesn't really matter, as long as they both like to do it in the same way, and they do eventually resolve their difficulties. What can be hard is when one person likes to shove troubles under the carpet and pretend they never happened, while the other likes a shouting match to clear the air.

CHECK IT OUT

Your kind of row

Many couples argue almost from day one, and even if you seldom fight at this stage of your relationship, you will undoubtedly find things that do rile you later on. Think about the patterns of disagreement in your relationship. Do you:

- Never row? ☐ ☐
- Have things you ought to sort out, but prefer to avoid doing it? ☐ ☐
- Repeat rows from a previous marriage or relationship? ☐ ☐
- Recognise that you have very different styles of tackling conflict that might make it hard to sort out problems? ☐ ☐
- Sometimes feel extremely angry with your partner? ☐ ☐
- Go round in circles when you disagree and never get anywhere? ☐ ☐
- Ever feel violent towards your partner, or fear that they feel violent towards you? ☐ ☐

Is there anything on the list that causes concern? Is this the way you'd like to go on resolving your differences in the future? If not, what needs to change?

Familiar Territory

It's very common for a couple's rows to follow the same old track almost every time. For instance:
- He accuses. She defends. He shouts. She shouts louder, then slams out, crying. He backs down and comforts her. They end up in bed.

or

- She blames. He denies. She carries on blaming, and adds a few other complaints for good measure. He clams up. She rages, then gives up. Hostility reigns for a couple of days, then things go on as if nothing had happened.

And so on. No doubt you can write your own scenario, but the trouble with stock rows like this is that partners switch on to auto-pilot when a bust-up starts and never get round to discussing the real issue properly, never mind clearing it up.

REAL LIVES

'Like it – or lump it.'

'It was our total inability to handle conflict that really did for my first marriage. The basic problem was that Paul was a workaholic. He stayed at the office until nine or ten every night, went in on Saturdays, brought work home on Sundays. We had no social life and eventually no sex life because he was always too exhausted. He would not admit that this was a problem. He said that he had to do it, and if I objected it meant that I wasn't supporting him in his career. Did I want him to stay at the bottom of the ladder all his life? No? Then I'd just have to put up with it. So rows either ended in stalemate, or, if I persisted, he became abusive and then violent. It was like it or lump it. He couldn't, or wouldn't, see the problem. After a year or two of this, I started staying late at work too, only for me the draw wasn't my job, but the guy in the next office. Inevitably we had an affair, which, although it only lasted a few weeks, was enough to make me see that there was real life to be had outside my marriage. I left.' *Maddy*

Counsellors say: *'People expect that their relationships can go on week in week out with no input from them, but they can't.*
Marriages need care and attention, an awareness of each other's concerns, and a willingness to adapt to meet your partner's needs.
Denying a problem, or refusing to address it, can seem like an easy

way out, especially if something is being demanded that you don't want to give. But denial solves nothing in the long term, and leaves the other partner feeling more and more frustrated and hurt.'

Row Tactics to Avoid

There are dozens of different ways to fight, but it's a fact that a great many of the approaches that people commonly use fail spectacularly to solve their disputes. The good news is that there are masses of excellent tactics you can use which guarantee much better results. But first look at this list of the no-hope approaches to disagreeing, and ask yourself honestly if you've ever used them.

Going on the defensive
Leaping to your own defence, justifying yourself aggressively:
'It's OK for you – I have to work far harder, so it's no wonder I forgot to buy the milk.' Partner feels under attack and may go on the defensive in response.

Retreating into silence
'When I try and get him to sort out the wedding guest list, he just grunts.' Avoiding conflict at all costs is maddening for the partner and can drive them into a disproportionate rage.

Refusing to admit that there's a problem
'I took a deep breath and said, "We need to talk about our problems," and he said, "Don't be daft, we haven't got any."' Partner feels unvalued and unheard, and may eventually give up trying to resolve problems, with result that things get worse.

Piling it on

Dragging in past battles, regardless of the current issue: *'The way you behaved at the party last night – that was so typical. You always get drunk and stupid whenever we go out.'* Partner feels under attack, may react defensively.

Showing contempt

Seeking to hurt and humiliate partner with well-chosen words of sarcasm or mockery: *'You think you look so great, don't you?'* May be a symptom of long-standing problems in the relationship. Highly destructive.

Getting very angry

Raging and shouting, usually out of proportion to what is being discussed, may hide underlying fear of rejection or of being controlled. Can be scary for partner, and does not allow for any reasoned discussion.

Becoming violent physically and verbally

Never acceptable.

Most people fall back on an overused battery of responses when they row, with the result that the same arguments are aired repeatedly but never resolved. If that ever happens to you – and it happens to most people some of the time – read on to discover more constructive ways to tackle friction, and finds methods that can move you forward instead of leaving you stuck and frustrated.

How does it look?

Make a drawing of how you feel when you and your partner have a 'typical' row. Do you feel like a mouse that's been cornered by a cat; like someone who's in the path of a steamroller; or as if you are beating your head against a brick wall or screaming into a void? Talk about what you find with your partner.

Visualising like this can help you to clarify what's going on when you argue. Now visualise the way you'd prefer to feel when you've had a row: would it be like a crane lifting a huge burden off you, or like the sun coming out?

Better Ways to Handle Conflict

It's easy to fall into the trap of seeing arguments as battles with a winner and a loser, yet it needn't be like that. In a marriage, ideally both people should come away from a row feeling as much like winners as possible – a win/win outcome. Adjusting to this line of thinking can be hard, especially if either of you is used to jockeying for position all the time in other areas of your life, especially at work.

A relationship founded on respect and trust won't work into the long term, though, if one partner always comes out of a row triumphant. They may feel good for a while because they got what they wanted but if their partner is repeatedly left feeling put-upon and resentful, steamrollered or coerced into a solution which doesn't really make them happy, then the future outlook isn't sunny.

THE BIG QUESTIONS

How can we handle rows more constructively?

Any of the following techniques really can make a difference. Many are simple, and even though some take more practice than others, in time you can make a habit of using them to improve the way you handle arguments.

- Choose a good time and place to talk, where you won't be interrupted or distracted, and when you are not too tired. Last thing at night is not a good time.
- Start gently. Don't kick off the discussion with an accusation or criticism. 'We need to talk about the best way to handle the regular bills,' is better than, 'The final demand's come for the phone again – why don't you ever remember to pay?'
- Listen carefully to what each other has to say. Don't assume that you know what your partner thinks. Be prepared to take on board your partner's feelings, and respond to them sensitively. Respect each other's views, even if you don't agree with them.
- Monitor your own responses and try to understand them. If your feelings seem out of proportion, think about why you are so upset. Does the present situation stir up memories of something that happened in the past, or when you were a child?
- Be sensitive to the physical warning signs, such as clenched fists or tears, that warn that you might be about to lose control, and give yourself time to calm down away from your partner. Make sure you go back and finish the conversation later.

- Stick to the point and don't drag in other topics or old grievances.
- Don't go silent, use tears or slam out of the room.
- Don't make threats.

Above all be flexible and willing to compromise. Be the first one to apologise. Look on a disagreement as a chance to work with your partner towards a good solution for both of you, rather than as an opportunity to get one over on them.

Use these techniques to stop wasting time and emotional energy on rows that go nowhere; become more able to discuss underlying grievances, and make sure that both of you get at least some of what you want every time.

SPEAKING FROM EXPERIENCE

'I know they say not to let the sun go down on your wrath, but our wrath often doesn't rise until well after midnight. Most of our big rows seem to start at bedtime, and can rage on into the small hours. We don't make it up before falling asleep. We retreat to opposite sides of the bed, sleep very badly with much gnashing of teeth, and stomp off in our different directions next morning. During the day, there's space and time to think about what's happened and realise that perhaps the other wasn't being so unreasonable. Almost always when we meet again in the evening we're ready to say sorry and have a more civilised discussion.' ADAM

Cultivating a willingness to compromise and be flexible means you'll be better able to accept that the best solution to any problem is one that satisfies both. It doesn't mean that you can never have what you want, that you must relinquish control to your partner, or that one of you must do all the giving. For more insights into how people argue and how to get better results from disagreements, try Susan Quilliam's book, *Stop Arguing, Start Talking* (see page 199).

The Power of the Past

Identifying the unhelpful strategies you use in rows is a good start, but before you can work on breaking the habit, it often helps to understand *why* you act the way you do. Do you come from a family of shouters or sulkers? When something went wrong, was the response a morose, 'Nothing ever goes right...'? Hands up anyone who's ever found themselves coming out with words – inappropriate, ridiculous or downright nasty – that they first heard within their family?

So often the reasons why someone reacts in a certain way to a certain situation lie in their past. Look back at relationships with your parents, with teachers, with previous partners and see where some of what you know about handling conflict has come from.

Children learn from example, and the lessons they pick up stick into adulthood. If your parents sorted out their differences amicably, then you know that you can solve problems without fighting. Even if you witnessed screaming matches, or heard raised voices from downstairs when you were in bed, as long as you also saw that your parents could work out their quarrels and carry on loving each other, you know that disagreements in themselves aren't necessarily harmful. It's how they get resolved that matters.

Likewise, past marriages or relationships that went wrong teach lasting lessons about conflict. If someone in your past dismissed your concerns and refused to discuss them, treated you like a child or bullied you, you'll have been left with a lot of expectations about what happens when people disagree. These, without your even being aware of it, may carry on into a new relationship.

Relate counsellor Julia Cole says, 'Sometimes, when people find a new partner very soon after a relationship break-up, it reassures them that nothing about them needed changing. Sadly, very often they discover that change *was* needed. Old problems resurface, and the same arguments they had in the past are repeated with the new partner. It's important to see the breakdown of a relationship as an opportunity to discover more about yourself. Identify what went wrong last time and take responsibility for your own contribution to the breakdown. It's hard, but unless something changes, there's a big risk that a new relationship will suffer from the same problems as the first.'

SPEAKING FROM EXPERIENCE

'In my upbringing there were few boundaries, and you could say pretty much what you felt like. Jyoti was brought up very traditionally in Africa, and had to show her parents a lot of respect and never speak out of turn. Sometimes it's been very hard. When I hear same-race couples talking about the things they argue about – he squeezes the toothpaste in the middle, that sort of thing – I think, that's easy compared with what we've had to face.'
PHIL

What do you know about conflict?

Write down a few phrases you've repeatedly said – or had said to you – over the years. They can be positive:

    'Let's try and sort this out, shall we?'

    'What would make you happy?'

or negative:

    'Don't be so stupid...'

    'Any more from you, and I'll...'

Once you recognise some of the things you've learned in the past about handling arguments, you can make efforts to rewrite your own script to include more of the positives. It's time to shake off the negative elements of the past. Remember, you are dealing with your partner now, not your parents, your boss or your big brother. What may (or may not) have worked in the playground or office, is probably totally inappropriate with your life partner.

Understanding Anger

Everyone gets angry from time to time, and in a long-term relationship you'll sometimes have to deal with your partner's anger as well as your own. Relate counsellor Christine Northam says, 'Getting angry isn't in itself a bad thing – it's normal. You can allow yourself not to like everything about your partner. Sometimes you will be very, very angry with them, and they with you. That's part of any marriage, but it must happen safely. You can be angry and still love each other.

'Anger is a powerful natural emotion that you can learn to use constructively once you've recognised and understood it. If your anger is ever too much, or threatens to overwhelm you, read books on managing anger, go on an anger management course, or get help from a counsellor or therapist.'

Think about the many different ways there are to express anger. For instance, you might show displeasure by going quiet, bingeing on food, getting drunk or staying late at work. All these are common responses, but how helpful are they in making a difference to your problems?

REAL LIVES

'I was so angry, it was frightening.'

When Gina and Chris were first married, they regularly had huge rows that usually ended with Gina smashing something or flouncing out in tears, while Chris clammed up completely and sat in silence while she raged. Gina said, 'I had ways of reacting to him that I see now were totally inappropriate. It was a re-run of the way I'd tried, rather successfully, to manipulate my parents when I was a bolshie teenager, trying to establish my rights in what was quite a restrictive set-up. In a way Chris reminded me of my father because he just kept his mouth shut when I was ranting on, and that was not the way to deal with the problem. All this was explored when we had counselling, and by talking about these past patterns, we were able to see what was happening and handle it better.'

Counsellors say: *'By becoming aware of influences from the past,*

people can gain much more insight into why they use destructive
and unhelpful ways of tackling problems. It takes courage to face
up to these things, and persistence to change them, but once you
realise what's going on, it is possible to adapt to new ways of
responding to a conflict – and if one person changes their
approach, their partner is very likely to change as well.'

Christine Northam has this suggestion if you find your anger sometimes seems out of proportion to a situation. 'It can be a very helpful starting point to think about what makes you angry. For instance, the anger you feel about your partner's behaviour or actions may actually be triggered by something that happened to you long ago. The more you understand why something sparks off your anger, the easier it will be to control it.'

When tempers are roused, and especially if someone has been drinking, it's not unusual for people who generally feel very good about their partner to fling something down, crash the door or otherwise express themselves violently. This kind of behaviour,

---

SPEAKING FROM EXPERIENCE

'Our biggest fights started whenever Jack tried to show me how to use the computer. It made me feel totally useless, and I'd lash out at him every time. Our counsellor helped me understand that because I'd been bullied and made to feel stupid at school, any attempt to show me how to do something took me straight back to those dreadful days and made me lash out in the anger and frustration I hadn't been able to show then.' ROSIE

---

though, is never justifiable, and can lead to physical violence, which brings fear and harm. When anger turns into violence, it becomes dangerous, and you need to do some honest thinking. If your partner's behaviour is unpredictable and out of control now, how will it be in the future? It could help you to talk to an expert. Some organisations offer helplines (see page 195 for details).

The Way You Feel Affects the Way You Row

Simple physical and emotional elements profoundly affect your ability to cope calmly with an upset.

- **The way you feel physically**
  Are you tired? Very tired? Most people cram a lot into their daily lives – so much so, that there's often not a lot of time or energy left to give to their partner. Or maybe you've just come home after a few beers. Alcohol can have a very bad effect on your mood and tolerance. Perhaps you're coming down with a cold, or feeling pre-menstrually grim. Any of these everyday physical factors can contribute to a disagreement that springs up out of nowhere – and grows alarmingly.

- **Other things going on in your lives**
  If you've already got a lot on your plate, it takes only one last little thing to tip the balance into a row. Something that at other times might have passed unnoticed can flare up like a rocket dropped into a smouldering bonfire. Be forgiving of yourself and each other. If you realise what is happening, say so: 'This is crazy. Why are we fighting about taking the rubbish out when you're going for a job interview tomorrow?'

Pre-wedding Rows

Couples who are approaching their long-awaited wedding day are often more than a bit snappy with each other. That's perfectly normal, and once the wedding is over and the heat is off, you can relax and ease up on each other.

It's time to worry, however, if the level of conflict is very high, unusually acrimonious, you feel intimidated or frightened, or if things are said that might indicate serious doubts about your marriage. If this happens, try to talk things through with someone outside the relationship whom you trust, preferably not a close family member, but a friend who is at more of a distance emotionally, or maybe a counsellor. See the section on Doubts and Fears, (page 36) for more on how to assess any anxieties, and what action to take.

Making Changes

Are there things you'd like to change about the ways you tackle disagreements? What would help you to get a better outcome? Changes are best made together, but you can still get results if just one of you starts responding differently. It's like a see-saw – if one person shifts, then so does the other.

Altering your pattern over disagreements in quite simple ways can have a knock-on effect on the rest of your relationship. For instance, if you know you tend to go on the defensive, and you resolve to be more open instead, your partner will become able to broach new areas for discussion without being afraid that you'll take off. However you usually tackle discord, you'll be able to pick up a few useful ideas from the list on page 92, which could help make bad rows less frequent and any quarrel far more manageable.

SPEAKING FROM EXPERIENCE

'We're getting married in a few weeks and are going mad trying to fix everything. We've only been living together for four months because we've spent the past three years running a long-distance relationship, with me working in Brussels and him here, just meeting up when we could. Now we're actually under the same roof it seems like the long honeymoon is over – before we're even married – and we're having so many rows. I feel deflated and depressed, and he's constantly grumpy and buries himself in computer games any chance he gets.' NADINE

'I hated being engaged. I sprouted a horrible rash all over my face and got dreadful headaches. We fought constantly, but carried grimly on to the big day, which – amazingly – we really enjoyed!' AMANDA

'Planning a wedding makes me feel crazy. I can't remember the last time we talked about anything else for more than ten minutes. There is just too much to do, and I'm really busy at work. Aargh – whose idea was this?' MICK

'I had very cold feet because we were having so many really horrible, bitter rows. I wish I'd paid my feet more attention – we were divorced 18 months later.' PAULINE

CHECK IT OUT

How to manage conflicts positively

Look through this list of positive tactics for handling disagreements. Which ones do you think are most important for you? Which do you not do at the moment but would like to try?

- Recognise that a problem exists, and needs sorting out.
- Be willing to look for a good compromise.
- Take a flexible approach in looking for solutions.
- Listen to each other and show you've really heard.
- Say how you feel.
- Forgive your partner/ask them for forgiveness.
- Say sorry.
- Take responsibility for your own feelings.
- Use humour to defuse a row.
- Agree not to row late at night or just before you go out.
- Pick a time to talk that is good for you both.
- Talk only when you are calm, stop if you get angry.
- Keep going until you do get to a good resolution.
- Resist the temptation to rush in with an instant fix.
- Accept that there won't always be a total solution, but keep trying to work something out.
- Recognise each other's emotions.
- Acknowledge each other's needs.
- Show that despite disagreeing, you still love and are committed to each other.

This is a list that you can come back to over the years, or when you feel as if you're stuck in a pattern of conflict that leads nowhere. Couples who both have high but realistic expectations of each other and their relationship, and are willing to do what's needed to meet those expectations, end up more content than couples who aim low because it seems easier.

Have no doubt, there will be conflict sooner or later in every relationship, but don't let that worry you unduly. Putting some effort into finding good ways to sort things out really does pay off.

Summary

- Check out how you approach arguments, and see where you could start to do it better.
- Understanding your history with conflict can help you to change.
- Anger can be scary, but needn't be destructive.
- It's not unusual to be on a short rein before the wedding. Go easy on yourselves.
- Simple tactics can work wonders when it comes to getting creative solutions to clashes.

5

Keep Your Sex Life Thriving

Lovemaking, the intimate sharing of physical and emotional energy that leaves you feeling totally satisfied and at peace with each other, is a wonderful way to reinforce your love, and deepen the bond between you. One of the great delights of married sex is that you can have it in so many ways: speedy and sexy, languorous and lingering, romantic, playful, raunchy – you've got a lifetime ahead to try them all.

THE BIG QUESTIONS

Do we share similar ideas about sex?

Couples who keep their sex lives simmering, even after the first heady excitement has worn off, usually have similar ideas and expectations about sex, and sex drives that are pretty much the same. Think about the questions in this list on your own, or share some or all of them with your partner. You might prefer to look at the questions separately and discuss anything that seems relevant afterwards.

'If you don't lust after your boyfriend, he's your best friend, not a prospective husband.' TRACEY COX

Sex and yourself

- Do you feel comfortable talking about sex?
- What kind of attitudes did your family have towards sex?
- What was the attitude in your family towards nudity, and towards showing physical affection with hugs?
- Can you tell your partner what you like them to do?
- Do you feel comfortable with your sexuality?
- How well do you know your own body? Do you feel OK about looking at your naked body, or touching yourself?
- For you, how long is too long to go without sex?
- How important do you think sex is within marriage?

Sex and your partner

- Are there things you still want to find out together about sex?
- Can your partner tell you what he or she likes you to do?
- Are you both happy with the amount of variety in your sex life?
- Is it a problem if one of you doesn't have an orgasm when you make love?
- Are there things one of you likes sexually that the other finds less enjoyable or unpleasant?
- Is it OK to have sex if only one of you really wants it?
- Does one of you want sex much more frequently than the other?
- Do you argue much about sex?

Stressful events, such as having a baby or taking on a responsible job, can affect libido. The important thing is to find a balance that suits you as a couple. Sex creates an intimate bond between two people, but how much sex you have is up to you: some couples can be happy having sex infrequently or not at all, while for others loss of sex would mean the end of the relationship.

Accepting Changes

Sex drive ebbs and flows, according to what else is happening in your lives. On holiday you might make love two or three times a day, while a fortnight later, when you're working hard on a big

---

SPEAKING FROM EXPERIENCE

'I'm from a strict Muslim background, whereas Kevin was brought up as a Catholic. Both faiths have quite tight role models for men and women, but that similarity didn't mean that we had a good sex life – quite the opposite. I'd always believed that a woman should be modest in bed, and I felt that it was wrong to show any enjoyment in sex. Kevin's upbringing had taught him that women should do what they're told in bed, but he was trying to throw that off and take a more modern approach, in which I was no help at all! He wanted me to be more responsive, but I found it impossible to let go. It's been very hard to shake off those strong influences from our families, and create a sex life for ourselves that is satisfying and pleasurable for us both.' JASWANDA

---

project, you might not have sex at all for a while.

The enjoyment you get from sex varies, too. Sex therapists reckon that for every ten times a couple make love, two times will be out-of-this-world wonderful, six will be just fine, thoroughly pleasurable, and the other two times – well, let's just say that they'll be less than the best. As long as the brilliant times are still happening often enough, there's no problem. After all, you've always got tomorrow night to have another go.

Everything that happens in your lives will have an impact on your sex life, so if you have a lot of changes – as people often do around the time they get married – your sex life will probably change too. If you're in the midst of a house move, for instance, or under a lot of stress at work, sex can suffer. And couples with babies and small children have to put lovemaking on the back-burner for a while.

If the frequency with which you have sex falls temporarily, there's often an obvious explanation. If sex floats off the agenda for too long, though, and you're not sure why, ask yourself if there are any other problems lurking under the surface. If you are angry with your partner, for instance, or afraid that something is going wrong, but can't talk about your fears, that will be enough to put you off sex for a while. Sex therapists always check out whether anything else is amiss in a couple's relationship before they start trying to 'cure' the sex problem. Sort out the other feelings, and very often the sex takes care of itself. That's worth remembering.

CHECK IT OUT

How well do you know each other sexually?

Answer these questions about your partner, either with them or, if
you prefer, privately. As well as thinking about how much you
know about your partner, think about what your own response
would be to each question. Then consider how closely your
responses and your partner's match.

My partner thinks:
- men should always initiate sex. ☐ ☐
- size matters. ☐ ☐
- sex without us both having an orgasm isn't real sex. ☐ ☐

My partner:
- likes his/her body. ☐ ☐
- doesn't like his/her body. ☐ ☐
- enjoys sharing his/her body with me. ☐ ☐

My partner:
- never has sexual fantasies. ☐ ☐
- has fantasies, but prefers to keep them private. ☐ ☐
- fantasises about me, and likes to share sexual
  fantasies with me. ☐ ☐

My partner's moods:
- How do you know if your partner is in the mood for sex?
- How do you know if your partner would like a cuddle, but
  doesn't want sex?

My partner:
- has had unpleasant sexual experiences in the past, which he/she still finds disturbing. ☐ ☐

My partner was brought up:
- able to be open about sex. ☐ ☐
- unable to discuss sexual matters within their family. ☐ ☐

My partner is turned on by:
- erotic films or magazines. ☐ ☐
- soft music, romance. ☐ ☐
- adventurous sex. ☐ ☐

Reflect on the answers to these questions. Is there anything you'd like to change? How could you do this?

REAL LIVES

'We ignored our problems, but they didn't go away.'

Malcolm: 'I'd been dissatisfied for a long time, but not for any particular reason. On the surface it was all perfect – lovely house, two kids, I had a good job. Our sex life was uninspiring, but we didn't fight about it, and I tried to ignore the unhappiness I felt inside.'

Evelyn: 'There'd been problems with sex when we lived together, but it didn't put us off getting married. I kept hoping things would sort themselves out, but they didn't, and last year we went for counselling. At that point I had to face up to the truth – I'd never really fancied Malcolm that much, but I loved him and was loath to hurt him, so I said nothing.'

Malcolm: 'The crunch came when my firm sent me to Madrid for two months, where I met and fell in love with another woman. Sex with her was wonderful, she made me feel desirable and loved. I came home and told Evelyn I wanted a divorce.'

Evelyn: 'It was a nightmare. I suggested we go back to the counsellor and try to sort things out again. Malcolm agreed to come, but we didn't get back together, although the counselling did help us to separate more amicably.'

Counsellors say: 'This case shows how important it is not to ignore problems and hope that they'll go away. Malcolm and Evelyn both knew that their sex life wasn't right before they got married. If they could have discussed the difficulties earlier on and sought help, rather than pretending everything was OK, they might have had a better sex life and been more able to talk about problems. It's vital to be honest, no matter how painful that is.'

SPEAKING FROM EXPERIENCE

'We've been together for 20 years, and our delight in sex is still just as strong as it always was. You do change a lot, of course. Lovemaking is different now. I suppose the initial fiery passion lasted five years or so. If ever one of us stopped feeling any desire, it would be awful.' MAGGIE

Sex for Life

Having a sex life that both of you enjoy, and where sex happens often enough to satisfy both of you, increases your chances of all-round marital happiness. It makes sense. If you're happy together in bed, then you've an underlying bond that cements your relationship in other ways. If your bed becomes a battleground and you turn away from each other too often, that rubs off on other areas of your lives as well. So how can you keep the flames burning, and make sure that your sex life doesn't get neglected?

- Don't get stuck into a sexual routine. Making love every Saturday night after 11 p.m. is not the way to achieve a teasing sense of delicious anticipation. Vary the when/how/where as much and as often as you can.

- Touch each other lots every day.

- Keep fit, take care of your body and your personal hygiene, and make yourselves enticing for each other.

- Aim for high energy levels in all areas of your lives. Get excited about everything, share that excitement with your partner, view sex as something to be relished.

- Talk about sex. Learn to leave embarrassment behind as your trust deepens. Try new ways of lovemaking, read sexy books or watch films together – do anything that you both enjoy and that turns you on together to enhance your sex life.

- Be kind and nice to each other, in bed and out of it.

- Keep closely involved. A partner who feels that you care deeply about their well-being is far more likely to want to make love than one who feels sidelined.

- It's been said that men who clean toilets get more sex. Doing the things that your partner wants you to do fosters good feeling, and good feeling fosters attraction and arousal.

Problem-solving

Many men occasionally find themselves having a problem with erections, or ejaculating sooner than they'd like. Similarly, women, and sometimes men, can go through phases where they find it really difficult to get aroused, or can't reach orgasm. Tiredness, working hard, having young children, being under stress, drinking too much – there's a long list of influences that can affect your sex life, so the occasional blip is nothing to worry about. As long as you can talk about it and reassure each other, problems often resolve themselves fairly easily.

If you have an ongoing problem:
- browse through the health and relationships sections at a bookshop for helpful books (see page 196 for suggestions).
- search the Internet for advice on sexual problems.
- visit a sympathetic GP, especially if you think difficulties stem from a health problem.
- Relate have specially trained psychosexual therapists who can help you to unravel the reasons for sex problems and put them right (see page 7 for more details).

Why do Affairs Happen?

Discovering that your partner has been unfaithful is devastating. Affairs are hugely threatening to a marriage, and infidelity is the most common reason cited for divorce. Surprisingly, though, an affair doesn't always mean the end of a marriage, and some couples survive an affair, and go on to become stronger.

REAL LIVES

'I missed out on casual relationships.'

Simon moved in with his first serious girlfriend when he was 22. That relationship broke up when he met his wife, Gilly, and he moved in with her straight away. They had been married for seven years, and had a toddler and a baby, when Simon came to Relate in a state of great concern and confusion. 'Lately I've felt so bored. I don't fancy Gilly any more, that's the bottom line, even though I still love so many things about her. Two weeks ago the inevitable happened. I met this gorgeous girl when I was away from home on business and we had a really wonderful night together – fun, no strings and physically great! I feel I've never really lived out the casual relationship phase most people have in their 20's. I don't want to lose Gilly, but I can't imagine living together for years with these feelings inside me.'

Counsellors say: *'It's understandable that Simon has these feelings, but it's a great pity that he has such deep regrets. Maybe Gilly has some of the same feelings, too. Casual sex appears so thrilling because there are no serious strings attached. Even when a relationship does have strings, like a mortgage, kids and so on, it is possible to have spicy, fun sex, but you have to make it a priority. Simon needs to think back to the start of his relationship with Gilly, and remember why they fancied each other. What did they do that felt special and exciting? Is there something they could try now? Could they find new things to do as a couple, not necessarily to do with sex, but interests that would take them into different surroundings? If Simon continues in counselling, he might be able to learn more about his feelings of missing out on an important stage of life, and put them into context.'*

Affairs don't just happen. They are very often a sign that something serious is amiss. Although some infidelities are all to do with the thrill of forbidden fruit, not every affair is centred on sex. Infidelity often stems from other dissatisfactions with the emotional side of a marriage, which lead one partner to look elsewhere for the love and understanding that is missing. Sex itself may be one of the least important facets of an affair.

So staying aware of *every* aspect of your married life, not just sex, and taking steps to remedy problems as soon as you notice them, is really important.

In her book *After the Affair* (see page 197), Relate counsellor Julia Cole lists some of the danger signs that one partner might be susceptible to an affair. These include:

- repeated arguments that are never resolved.
- not talking about important areas of your relationship.
- struggling with a crisis, such as illness or bereavement.
- having a dull but busy lifestyle that doesn't give you much time for each other.
- sex problems that you haven't talked about.

These are the kinds of problem that can creep up gradually and make people susceptible to straying. You can protect your marriage against affairs by:

- cultivating trust through being honest and open about your feelings.
- building on your commitment to each other (see page 40).
- giving yourself 'permission' to make your relationship a priority without feeling guilty.
- facing up to problems.
- agreeing together on boundaries of relationships with other people, for instance, it is OK to see someone of the opposite

sex on your own socially?

- telling your partner that you care for them, and demonstrating it by the way you behave.
- not being complacent about your partner's fidelity, or taking it for granted.
- avoiding intimate friendships with people you fancy.

THE BIG QUESTIONS

Could infidelity be a serious threat to our relationship?

Read the statements below and tick whether you agree, or disagree.

	Agree	*Disagree*
• We have talked about what it would mean if either of us was unfaithful.	☐	☐
• We have a strong commitment to each other.	☐	☐
• We are good friends.	☐	☐
• We don't spend enough time together.	☐	☐
• I sometimes wonder how much my partner really cares about me.	☐	☐
• I trust my partner completely.	☐	☐
• We are good at talking about problems as and when they arise.	☐	☐
• We can talk about sex.	☐	☐
• We have a firm belief in the long-term future of our relationship.	☐	☐
• It's important to be involved in each other's lives and to spend time together.	☐	☐

Think about these statements. What would infidelity mean in your marriage? What are the implications if you and your partner find each totally trustworthy, or if you don't? Beware of complacency. Understanding that even the most devoted spouse might sometimes be tempted can help to ensure that you do everything possible to make your own relationship the most attractive element in both your lives.

The fact that infidelity almost always arises from other problems within a relationship, underlines the guiding rule for a successful marriage: take care of your relationship, safeguard it, put time into it. Talk to each other and keep talking because talking brings you closer. Don't ignore problems. Taking a positive and active approach to keeping your relationship strong and able to face up to the challenge of change is vital.

Remember that sex is all about showing love and having fun. Lighten up, let yourselves laugh together and enjoy yourselves. Lovemaking is a great way to express affection and acceptance, give and receive pleasure, and stay in touch with the sensual side of your relationship.

Summary

- Keep the excitement going.
- Go with the flow and take on board any changes.
- Develop a deep trust and learn to talk openly about sex.
- Affair-proof your marriage.
- Don't take sex too seriously – have fun!

6

Avoid the Money Minefield

Money is the fuse that ignites more marital rows than any other issue. Why? Very often feelings about finances change when you marry. Events that have a far-reaching effect on your cash-flow and spending habits, such as buying a house together, or having a baby, often coincide with marriage. Couples who've previously jogged along keeping their monies more or less separate can face a steep learning curve about each other's attitudes to saving and spending. If you can learn to see eye to eye when sorting out money concerns, you'll be doing yourselves an enormous favour.

Money Angst

Why is money such a troublemaker? It's not just how much you have, although scraping by is very stressful – the less money you have, the more likely you are to fight over what little there is. Even more important, though, is how you manage your assets.

- **Spending priorities**
  Wanting to spend money on different things is a common cause of wrangles. He wants a new car, she wants a great holiday.

- **Inequality**

  Very often one partner brings home substantially more than the other. Even if this isn't so at the start of a relationship, when children arrive, one person's income, most often the woman's, takes a nosedive for a while. Imbalance can cause strife because money so often equates with who has control. If the prime earner's attitude is, 'I earn the money – I decide how to spend it,' it's an open invitation to disagreement and resentment from the partner who feels stripped of power because they earn less.

- **Secrecy**

  It can be tempting to keep quiet about money concerns, especially if, say, you've overspent or got into debt and know your partner would disapprove. Secrets like this within a relationship can be very damaging. See page 70 for hints on how to come clean with your partner. You'll also need to try and stop the same thing happening again.

SPEAKING FROM EXPERIENCE

'For the first couple of years we were married, money wasn't a problem. We both had good jobs, there was plenty of money, and I wasn't bothered about how much he paid to his ex-wife as maintenance for their three children. Then we had a kid of our own and I stopped working. Our income dropped by a third overnight, but the maintenance payments didn't. Rationally, I knew it was right that he should support the children, but I felt very resentful about the money going out. I felt I was being driven back to work sooner than I wanted by his ex-wife.' SALLY

- **Money in second families**

  If either of you has been married before, and especially if you have children from a previous relationship, money is highly likely to be the source of friction about topics such as:

  - how much is paid to a first family, and how much is spent on the new one.
  - money as manipulator, withheld to punish a former partner, or demanded by them to control the new family.
  - money spent lavishly in a bid to relieve guilt, or 'buy' the love of a child from whom you are separated.

What's Underneath a Money Problem?

Money is a potent symbol of many things. When handled well, it shows a high level of trust and mutual security in a marriage. Managed badly, though, it can indicate distrust, coupled with lack of freedom or power. Rows that break out about money often hide underlying fears of losing control or being kept in the dark.

THE BIG QUESTIONS

Do we have similar attitudes to money?

Check through this list for yourself and get your partner to do the same. Then compare notes, and see how closely your answers coincide.

How do you handle your earnings?
- Budget carefully and always know how much is in your account.

- Keep spending until the cash card stops working.
- Save something every month.

Suppose you won the lottery. Would you:

- Spend, spend, spend.
- Invest all your winnings to give yourself an income for life.
- Give generously to friends, family and charity.

What's the best way to handle your finances as a couple?

- You have your bank account, I'll have mine.
- Put everything into one account together.
- Keep some separate and pool the rest.

Whose job is it to pay the bills and keep tabs on your money?

- His.
- Hers.
- You do it together.

Is it OK to run up credit card debts?

- As long as you pay it all off every month.
- Up to the limit, and pay it off as and when you can.
- Never, it's the path to ruin.

If money is limited, what's most important?

- A decent holiday every year – we need it.
- Saving regularly, without fail.
- Keeping up our present standard of living, even if it means we can't save.

How much can you spend without checking with your partner?

- As much as I like.
- Always check with purchases over £50 (or another agreed sum).
- What I spend is none of their business.

> *'Please Lord, let me prove to you that winning the lottery won't spoil me.'* VICTORIA WOOD

These are just a few areas where couples can come unstuck if they differ over money. Think about your attitudes. They were probably shaped by the spending and saving habits in your family, and these may well be out of date. For instance, credit is much more readily available now than it was a generation ago, which has led to many changes in people's spending patterns. Is there anything on this list that you want to talk to your partner about? Did you feel able to go through the list with your partner? If not, why not? Think about your answers.

Expectations About Money

Once again, history – your personal history – has a part to play in your attitudes towards money. For instance:

- In your family, was money a cause of arguments? Who controlled the spending? Did the system work OK?
- Have you fought about money in previous relationships? If so, has it left you feeling nervous if your current partner shows signs of wanting to take financial risks, for example, or wants to curb your spending in some way?

These kinds of experience can have a powerful influence on your money habits, and not always one that is useful or good. Take a minute to think about how money has been handled in your past, and how you would like it to be different now.

'I didn't know about her debts.'

When Sam met Lally, he was very impressed by the way she looked. She had designer clothes, an immaculate flat and a good job in the City. 'What I didn't know was that she also had staggering debts. She had three credit cards which she had run up to the limit, plus store cards galore. She was drowning in a sea of debt and covering it up. Even when I moved in with her after a few months, she was careful to hide the mail – and she kept on spending. It wasn't until we were planning our wedding that I found out, when her credit card was refused in a store. I was already a bit suspicious, and when we got home I asked to see her credit card statements. At first she refused, but then she got them out and sat there while I totted it up: she owed more than £20,000 by then. I realised that she'd lied to me about money, and that I didn't know her nearly as well as I'd thought I did. The wedding was cancelled. I'm not sure if I'll ever regain enough trust to make the relationship work.'

Counsellors say: *'It's a golden rule that intimate relationships depend on a high level of trust. Having a secret means that you're withholding something of yourself from your partner, which prevents the two of you from fully connecting. This applies just as much to secrets about money, as it does to secrets about anything else in your life. Openness and honesty are vital.'*

Another thing to remember is that money, like all other aspects of life, doesn't remain static. Couples who've been used to an independent life with a good income and financial freedom, can find that settling down together and taking on commitments such as a shared mortgage and family call for a big adjustment. If you already have children, you'll know what a hole they make in your bank balance, while if you're planning to start a family, you'd be wise to do some research into the real costs. Thinking about what the future might hold, and talking, even very loosely, about how you'd cope financially can alert you to possible problems before they grow.

CHECK IT OUT

Where does your partner stand on money?

Answer these questions about your partner. They can answer the questions, about you too if you like.

- How much do they earn?
- What proportion of their income do they spend every month?
- And how much do they save?
- What do they regard as essential spending?
- What would be a real luxury for them?
- Do they take financial risks?
- What are their views on credit?
- Is money very important to them?
- Do they give to charity?
- Is it easy to talk to them about financial matters?
- If not, why not?
- What does your partner think about your attitudes towards money?

Are there gaps in what you know about your partner? Does this bother you? Are there other things you don't know about your

partner? It's very common for couples to have different attitudes
towards money, and it's important to start to understand these
now and tackle any problems they provoke so that there are no
misunderstandings later on. The more freely you can talk, the
more likely it is that your relationship will work well. Pre-nuptial
agreements, widely used in the USA and continental Europe, but
not legally recognised in England and Wales, do not appeal to
everybody, but can have their uses. They are signed before
marriage and itemise the financial arrangements to be made in
the event of a divorce. If the idea seems useful to you, you might
find that making one, even informally, helps focus on where
money problems might arise in future.

Getting to Grips with Money Problems

If money is giving you grief now, or you suspect that it might in future, what can you do?

Before you even start, remember that money is a thorny subject, and can prove very hard to talk about. Sorting out problems demands a high level of trust, openness and flexibility. Be prepared for it not to be easy, and give it time. You probably won't solve all your money problems in one session, so take it bit by bit.

- Agree on some rules for how you deal with money. If you are pretty much in agreement, then these might never need to be spelt out – they'll just evolve of their own accord. But if you find money a frequent bone of contention, it could help to settle on some ground rules, such as:

- how much each of you can spend without checking with the other.
- how much credit you can run up.
- what savings you're aiming to accumulate.
- Consider drawing up a monthly budget so that you can see what's coming in and where it's disappearing to.
- Come clean about debts and make plans together for clearing them and preventing any more from mounting up.
- Try to find answers that suit you both to questions such as:
  - Who will pay for what?
  - How will we manage bank accounts and savings?
- If one partner's income went down, how would we reorganise our finances? How would we provide money for the partner with less income to cover personal outgoings? If one of us stopped earning, would we still have an equal say on how money is managed?
- For second families, talk through the financial arrangements that are already in place and try to troubleshoot problems. Is there anything about these arrangements that has caused problems in the past? Were you happy with how those were resolved? What will happen if you have children, or if your income is reduced for another reason, such as redundancy or a return to study?

Money isn't something that can be sorted out once, then forgotten about. As circumstances change, you'll need to renegotiate, probably many times. See Keep Talking, page 59, and Resolve Conflict, page 75, for more suggestions about how you can start talking amicably about money, now and in the future.

Summary

- Work out where you both stand on money matters. Do your best to agree.
- Act to resolve problems before they become hot prospects for a row.
- Identify the areas where you differ and look for good compromises.
- Talk through your spending and saving priorities, and revisit them whenever something changes in your lives.
- Be open and upfront with each other when you talk about money.

7

Share the Ups and Downs of Parenting

For the majority of couples, children are very much part of the picture of being married. Being a parent alters your perspectives and your priorities. Children bring love and happiness, fun and a sense of purpose. Even though anxieties, frustrations, hard graft and heartache are part of the same package, making children a part of your lives brings immense rewards.

Many couples get married having already had children together, and a lot also have children from previous relationships to consider. Others might marry during their first pregnancy or hope to conceive fairly soon after the wedding. Having children together sometimes marks a different level of commitment, and is the moment when cohabiting couples decide to marry.

Deciding to Have a Child

Having a child is a shared responsibility, as well as a shared delight, and the decision to become parents must be a wholehearted and joint one. Children will change your lives in lots of ways. Parenting can be tough on your marriage at times, but

'Sometimes when I look at my children I say to myself, "Lillian, you should have stayed a virgin." ' MIZ LILLIAN CARTER, MOTHER OF US PRESIDENT JIMMY CARTER

coming through the challenging times together can also bring you a lasting closeness.

THE BIG QUESTIONS

What do we think about being parents?

Having children is a long-term undertaking, which has profound effects on your relationship. Talk through some of the decisions and dilemmas that couples commonly face on the road to parenthood, either with a view to the future or in the light of an existing family.

- Have you talked about having children, and are you agreed on your hopes for having a family?
- If you are agreed that you would both like to have children:
  - Do you agree on how many you would like?
  - When would you like to have your first child?
  - And when would you hope to have subsequent children?
- Have you thought about who will take responsibility for childcare?
- How will you manage financially?
- What will happen with your jobs?
- Does one of you not want children, or is one of you undecided?
  - If so, how are you going to cope with this difference?

- Suppose you wanted children, but found you couldn't have them? Would this:
  - cause big problems – having children is very important to us?
  - be something we'd adapt too – there are other things in life apart from children?
  - definitely put us on track for fertility investigations, despite the expense and emotional strain involved?
- If you already have children:
  - are you agreed on whether you want any more children?
  - are your financial arrangements working OK?
  - do you see eye to eye on the children's upbringing?
  - are you both reasonably happy with the balances you've struck between work and parenting?

SPEAKING FROM EXPERIENCE

'We've lived together for three years and we're getting married to put our relationship on a more permanent basis by standing up in front of our family and friends and saying, "Look, I want to spend the rest of my life with this person." I don't see Al and I suddenly changing the way we organise the household or our little habits just because we're husband and wife. One thing that will change, however, is that we will be trying to start a family in the next year or so. Call us old-fashioned but we both wanted to wait until we were married before we had a baby – that goes back to that whole thing about permanency.' CAROLINE

Many of these are difficult questions, often without clear-cut answers. One thing is certain, though. Having children will change things between you. If one of you is uncertain, or you are wondering if a pregnancy would hold together a rocky relationship, think twice. Talk it over, and if you can't talk it over, ask yourself why. Try to reach a decision that feels right to you both.

Research has shown that when both partners want a baby, their relationship is more able to thrive during the testing early years of parenthood. If only one of you is keen on the idea, though, having

---

SPEAKING FROM EXPERIENCE

'The worst personal trauma in my marriage was when my daughter managed to scald herself all over her face and down the front of her tiny torso at the tender (literally) age of six months, by spilling a jug of boiling water. Her delicate skin peeled off in ribbons. She could have died from loss of body fluid. Seeing her swathed in bandages, two little eyes peeping out, I thought my heart was breaking. She was hospitalised for a week, but it was many weeks before we learnt she wouldn't need skin grafts. Mercifully, thanks to the body's incredible power of healing, she recovered fully and is now a beautiful, unmarked 19-year-old, with no memory of the event. My husband's no-nonsense, stoical approach to life helped me, with all my feelings of self-blame and guilt, through my darkest moment as a mother. That's what "good marriage" is all about.' LIZ

---

children can pile on unbearable pressure. In the Relate book *Babyshock!* (see page 197), counsellor Lucy Selleck points out how risky it is to go ahead with a pregnancy if only one partner wants a child. 'Often the woman hopes the man will change his mind when the pregnancy becomes a *fait accompli*. Sometimes that does happen, but people don't necessarily change their minds. If you are at odds over whether or not to have a baby, don't assume that things will change. They might, but they might not.'

REAL LIVES

'We fell into marriage without thinking it through.'

Andy, 30, who had a small son from a previous marriage, and Nicole, 23, had been together for just over a year. They spent most week nights at Nicole's flat, but Andy's son usually came to his father's flat for weekends, and Nicole would take some time out for herself. This arrangement worked well, but then Nicole got pregnant accidentally.

'Our reaction – to get married and move in together properly – was a knee-jerk. We didn't talk it through, we just did it. Within weeks we were fighting all the time, both of us missed our own space, and having Andy's son at weekends made me feel unbearably crowded. We staggered on until the baby was born, but after three months nothing was better, so I took the baby and moved in with my mum and dad for a while. It was drastic, but it helped us realise that we did still want to be together, so now we're looking for somewhere bigger to live, where we won't feel so hemmed in.'

Counsellors say: *'When couples, especially younger ones, marry quickly and have a baby in the first year, or maybe marry because the woman is already pregnant, they haven't given their own relationship a chance to grow. Things soon go wrong because they feel so trapped, and these relationships have a high risk of breaking up.'*

If You Don't Want Children

A growing minority of couples decide not to have children, and if current trends continue, one woman in five who is now approaching 30, will not have had children by the time she is 45.

For some couples parenthood has simply never appealed, others would prefer to concentrate on a career, while for some financial reasons are the deciding factor. Counsellor Christine Northam says, 'Sometimes an unwillingness to have children can be the result of an unhappy childhood. Make sure you understand fully why it is that you've made this decision.' Whatever the reasons, you'll need to talk them over and reach a considered choice together, which feels right to both of you.

One thing to be aware of is that major decisions like this sometimes need to be revisited and reaffirmed. People can change their minds, particularly when their peer group start producing children. At this stage, if you've grown used to the idea of not having children, it can be very hard to turn that decision around, especially for a woman faced with relinquishing a job that may have been very important to her. As a couple, you need to stay aware of each other's changing needs and desires, and remain able to review past decisions openly and honestly if necessary.

If You Can't Have Children

Many people would love to have children, but life hasn't worked out that way. Perhaps they've paired up with someone who already has children and doesn't want – or can't afford – to have more. For women, the biological clock may have run out before they met the right partner. And, of course, as many as one couple in six tries unsuccessfully to conceive.

For these couples, being unable to have children in a world where most people do become parents is extremely hard.

Most couples who haven't conceived after a year or so of trying seek medical help. A number of treatments are available, and which one is suggested depends on the reasons underlying the infertility, although these too can be hard to pinpoint. For many,

---

SPEAKING FROM EXPERIENCE

'Imagine walking past a cake shop filled with the most delicious-looking cakes. You really want one, but you can't go in, and no one can tell you why you can't go in. All you can do is look, while other people go in and come out with those lovely cakes. That's what it's been like for me, not being able to have children. We tried for a baby for seven years, had different treatments, but none of them worked. At last we gave up, and now we're a few years on, but I'm still adjusting, it's an ongoing process. The feeling of loss is always there. I'd say we've become closer because of what we have gone through. Your life can become a lot fuller in other ways. It's how you try and make it, you have to be very positive. That process, though, is very gradual.' KARIN

'Zeb and I were very definite that we both wanted children. I remember we planned to have our first child within 18 months of getting married, and another one 18 months after that. I was 33, so we didn't want to hang around for too long. It didn't occur to either of us that there might be a problem, but the months went by and still I wasn't getting pregnant. Eventually I went to my doctor, who referred us for fertility tests, but the clinic couldn't identify any problem, and took ages to settle on a suitable treatment. Meanwhile, precious time was rolling past. I was prescribed drugs to stimulate ovulation and at long last I did conceive. Madeleine was born when I was 37, but whether or not we'll be able to have that second child, who knows?' MIRIAM

it's the start of a difficult and sometimes lengthy procedure, with no guarantee of success at the end.

The first port of call should be your GP, who can refer you for tests and explain more about the treatment options available. While some treatments are fairly simple, others, such as IVF and the use of donated sperm or eggs, should be given careful thought before you embark on them. These treatments are not right for everyone, and you need to take expert advice and talk the issue over together, at length, before deciding. Some couples who find they cannot have children, consider adopting a child, but this in itself is not a straightforward process. See pages 192–193 for organisations who offer support to couples who are having infertility treatment, or who have decided to discontinue treatment and adjust to the idea of a future without children.

Managing Work, Life and Kids

Achieving everything – a good job, children, a fulfilling life – is a tough goal, but one that many couples set themselves. It's not wise to try and spread yourself too thinly, though, and you'll have to work out some compromises. Research has shown, for instance, that women who go back to work full time rather than part time after having a baby have a higher risk of marriage breakdown. Some women do manage well, but it pays not to underestimate what's involved in juggling two big responsibilities.

Men also have problems getting the balance right. One counsellor saw a couple who had both had demanding full-time jobs. When the first child arrived, the husband was incensed that his wife wanted to go part time – why should she get the pleasure of time with the children, while he was stuck in the office earning a living for them all?

Other pressures can come from parents or in-laws who don't share your views on working and raising a family. Try your best to win their understanding about your ideas because having the support of your family can be an enormous benefit. Even if they don't roll up their sleeves and take care of the children for you, just hearing that they think you're doing a great job can help to keep you going.

Working out a good balance of responsibility over childcare is something that causes problems for many couples. Sorting out solutions is a matter of trial and error. What works well when children are tiny won't be so good once they're at school. It's all a balancing act. See Prioritise Your Relationship (page 135) for help on how to share out your time effectively.

Bringing Up Children

Once you have children, you'll take on the roles of parents together. Almost certainly, there will be areas of parenting where you don't agree. Talk about your own childhoods and your expectations of how children will be brought up. There are masses of questions you can ask, such as:

- What are our views on discipline?
- How hands-on will the baby's dad be?
- Is it OK to leave babies and children with babysitters while we get some time for ourselves?
- What kind of schooling should our children have?

You probably won't be able to answer many of these questions until you actually need to address them for your own children, but thinking about the issues that might arise can be a useful way to point up any differences that could be tricky to negotiate later on.

SPEAKING FROM EXPERIENCE

'Our views on raising children came from opposite ends of the spectrum. Amerjit had been brought up with no set bedtime, eating what he wanted, making lots of noise. I came from a stricter family, where I'd had to eat up my dinner, go to bed when I was told and so on. We had completely different expectations of what being a parent involved. We've got two small boys now, and every day there's something that we don't agree on, but we have to work it through, without being confrontational.' KRISTIN

Children from Previous Relationships

More than a quarter of under-16s will experience their parents' divorce, while others will witness the break-up of cohabiting parents, or lose a parent through death. Since over half of divorced parents remarry, huge numbers of children will also be involved when their parents set up with a new partner.

There are dozens of different kinds of stepfamilies.

- You might have young children living with you permanently, or teenagers who visit only occasionally.
- Children may come to you, or you might go off for days, weekends or holidays to be with them.
- You could have just one stepchild to consider, or several children of different ages and from different relationships to take into account.

If you have reached the stage of contemplating marriage where children from previous relationships are involved, then undoubtedly you will already have come face to face with some of the issues. Spending time with the children and getting time and privacy for yourselves, juggling a divided life, fixing holidays, building a relationship with the children, making arrangements with an ex-partner – all these are part of the maze that new couples have to negotiate.

You may feel that you have already crossed many of the bridges. But deciding to marry can alter things. It draws a definite line under what went before, and states your commitment loud and clear. It says to the children that this is for real, and there is now no chance of their parents getting back together. It says to an ex that what's past is past, and it's time now for things to move on.

Remember, a stepfamily only ever comes into being because

somewhere along the line there has been a major loss, and loss inevitably brings pain. Even if the two adults who are at the core of the new family feel good about it, it doesn't follow that the children will feel the same, and they may resent the new arrangement that they see as being foisted on them. Their anger, jealousy and pain can be expressed as tantrums, bad behaviour at school, emotional withdrawal or in a hundred other ways. Relate Family Counselling (see page 7) can offer help if big changes within your family are causing disputes and stress.

SPEAKING FROM EXPERIENCE

'Every weekend there would be Bill's kids on the doorstep, wearing dirty clothes and with nothing to change into. We were supposed to have a standing arrangement that they came on Friday at six and were picked up at midday Sunday. His ex wouldn't speak to me – nor to Bill, if she could help it – but almost every week she'd vary the arrangement, tell the kids that she'd be picking them up three hours late or whatever, and leave it up to them to tell us. And even then she'd never arrive on time. I used to get angry with Bill – why couldn't he control her – but in the end I twigged: she was trying to cause a rift between us. Using the kids was her only way to get the upper hand. After that I found it easier to be more laid back about the whole thing and now, two years down the line, she's met someone else too, and the messing about has stopped.'
CINDY

CHECK IT OUT

Map your life

Draw a map of your new, extended family. Place yourselves in the centre, with a series of circles spreading out from you like ripples. Use stickers or draw figures to show where you see each person in the family as being in relation to you. Then draw lines connecting the people: they can be thin lines for a tenuous connection, jagged ones to show conflict, wavy lines to show uncertainty, or you can use different colours to show the type of connection. Visualising like this can help you to see where conflicts and tensions might lie. Talk about what you have discovered. How would you like the map to look? If you like, draw another 'ideal' map. What would the consequences be if this new map became the reality? What could you do to move towards achieving your ideal map?

Finding a role

One important aspect of forming a relationship with your partner's children is finding a role for yourself that works well.

- Don't try to replace the missing parent.
- It's not necessary, or possible, to re-create the old, nuclear family. Instead, you need to create something new, that works for all of you.
- There's no need to be totally emotionally involved with your stepchildren. Taking a step back can help you feel less overwhelmed.
- If you, the new couple, decide to have children of your own, be prepared for this to alter the relationship with the existing children.

'I can't shake off the guilt.'

Yvette's two teenagers from her first marriage live with her and Henry, her second husband. Henry also has two teenage children, who live with his ex-wife. Henry says, 'I feel very guilty being more closely involved with my stepchildren than with my own children. I feel I can't get too close to Yvette's two because mine will think it isn't fair. I see mine every other week, and we do talk and email in between times, but it's not the same as living under the same roof. I'm missing so much and I'm always going to feel bad about not being there enough. Another problem for us is that Yvette's kids don't go out much, so we never get time alone in the evenings.'

Counsellors say: 'There's a lot to accept when you take on a stepfamily, not least having to establish a working relationship with possibly bolshie kids who wish you weren't there. Henry accepts that he is always going to feel regret and guilt from not being with his own children. He shouldn't let these feelings stop him having as much contact with them as is feasible in order to maintain a close relationship into adulthood.

'One easier element within this family is that Yvette's children are already in their teens and will probably move on in a few years. In the meantime Henry and Yvette must go out alone together regularly. In this way they can demonstrate to the children the importance of their relationship as a couple. Couples who take on a family of young children can find it much harder to get privacy and time for themselves to nurture their own relationship – vital if you are coping with the demands of so many other people on top of your own needs.'

THE BIG QUESTIONS

Can we handle becoming a stepfamily?

Whatever your situation, meshing children from past relationships into a new family is seldom straightforward. Ask yourselves these questions together, and think about the answers.

- Have you told the children of your plans to marry?
- Ideally, all the adults involved should sit down together and work out the best arrangements for the children. The children should also be asked how they feel about these arrangements. Will that be possible for you?
- Even when you have set up some arrangements, can you accept that you may have little control over the way they are implemented? This applies whether you are a new spouse receiving children's visits, or whether you are sending your children to your ex for the weekend.
- How will you keep the channels of communication open? It's vital to do this somehow, even if it gets very difficult. Would you be able to have frequent contact in person or on the phone that allows you to talk openly about matters concerning the children?
- Can you keep the children's best interests in mind all the time? How easy will it be to do that?
- How flexible can you be?
- What will happen about taking holidays and celebrating birthdays, Christmas and other festivities?
- Have you worked out a role for yourself with your partner's children?
- Have you discussed how you will handle day-to-day life when the children are with you?

- Who will make decisions about and be responsible for:
  - discipline?
  - setting boundaries on behaviour?
  - spending on the children?
  - important aspects of the children's lives, such as schooling?
- How will you get time for yourselves as a couple?
- Do you plan to have children of your own? How do you envisage them fitting in with the other children?

Creating a new family is a big commitment and takes a lot of hard work. It doesn't happen magically. Problems concerning stepchildren can put a big strain on a relationship, which is probably one reason why second marriages break up more often than first ones. For the sake of all the children involved, as well as the adults, it pays to think long and hard about all the implications of setting up a stepfamily. Accept that life won't be perfect. Allow yourselves to make mistakes, but learn from them if you can. See page 7 for details of Relate Family Counselling, and page 191–195 for other help organisations that can offer advice and information to stepfamilies.

Enjoying Parenthood

Whether you are planning to have kids of your own together, are taking on a stepfamily, or both, some of the time you'll be having to draw on all your reserves of patience and maturity. What you'll get in return is the fun and laughter of family life, the sense of pride and pleasure that parents have in their children, the underpinning of a shared love for the children that can enhance and enrich your marriage over the years.

CHECK IT OUT

How well would we manage being parents?

Look at these questions together and see where you agree or
disagree.

	Agree	Disagree
• I'm looking forward to having children with my partner.	☐	☐
• Spending lots of time together, just the two of us, is very important.	☐	☐
• I want to be the most important person in my partner's life.	☐	☐
• Having children won't alter our lives that much.	☐	☐
• I'm happy to share my partner with his/her children from a previous relationship.	☐	☐
• Freedom to go out when I like is very important to me.	☐	☐
• It's vital that I get eight hours sleep a night.	☐	☐
• My work is the most important element of my life.	☐	☐
• Frequent sex is central to our relationship.	☐	☐
• I'd like our relationship to stay just as it is.	☐	☐
• My partner copes well if I'm tired or feeling under the weather.	☐	☐
• I think we'd make good parents.	☐	☐

*Reflect on your answers. Having children is one of the biggest
changes that happens in most marriages, and while it brings
many positive benefits, you need also to think about how you'd
cope with having less freedom and less time for each other.*

Parenthood is demanding, there's no denying it, but family life is certainly never dull. Faced together, even the most testing of family problems offer you a chance to deepen your relationship with each other and with your children.

Summary

- Having a baby should be a mutual decision, something you both really want to do.
- Think carefully through the choice to remain childless.
- Infertility can be very stressful and hard. You'll need to be strong for each other.
- The way you were brought up will influence the way you raise your own family.
- Building a new family that includes children from previous relationships is very worthwhile. Be prepared for it to take a long time and a lot of maturity.
- Children can enrich your lives beyond measure. Relax and enjoy family life together.

8

Prioritise Your Relationship

Early on in a relationship, it's easy finding hours and hours for each other. Other plans get dropped or shelved, and love takes priority. Once past that stage of mutual immersion, though, the demands of life – long hours at work, friends, family, home and garden, children, interests and hobbies – start munching away at the time you have to spend together. It can happen without your even noticing, but failing to give each other enough time erodes the strongest relationship, just as surely as pounding waves wear away a cliff.

Does it matter? Relate counsellor Annie Wilson thinks it does. 'Time spent together is so important. If you are too wrapped up in kids/chores/work, the relationship shrivels and dies. It is a delicate balance, though, to be free enough to follow your own interests, but still to have enough time to nurture your relationship.'

How Much Time Do You Need?

Couples are very different in their needs and in the ways their lives are organised. Getting the balance about right can be a challenge, as these three couples have found.

- **Rob and Christine** have set up a business together. Christine says, 'We're in each other's company 24/7. Every aspect of our lives – work issues, domestic stuff, the children – is shared. It's very exciting to be doing this together, but in the long term we aim to have other people working for us, so that we don't have to do it all ourselves, and so that we can both get time away from the business, doing things that we used to enjoy, like tennis.'

- **Tricia and Ray** used to lead very separate lives. Tricia says, 'I looked after our two small children and worked part time, while Ray was often away travelling with his job. He used to be gone for ten days or more at a time. We found it very hard, we missed each other so much, and it took ages for the children to get used to him again when he came back. Now he's switched to another job, which means that although he's away a couple of nights each week, the rest of the time he can work from home. We've taken a drop in income, but it's been well worth it in order to spend more time together.'

- **Melanie and Dave** don't have children. Both work full time and keep up with separate friends and interests. Dave says, 'We used to see friends separately in the evenings and at weekends. I often worked on into the evening, too. It got so that the only time we could catch up with each other was on holiday, and in the end I was wondering what was the point of being married. Now we've decided to keep one day at the weekend completely free for us, and spend a minimum of two evenings a week together, every week. At last we have a chance to chat and relax together instead of endlessly rushing around.'

What suits one couple could be the worst possible lifestyle for another, so there is no off-the-peg formula. What you can do is work within the constraints of your lives to find the level of togetherness that suits you both. Then make it a top priority to preserve those times together, that contact, no matter what. Drifting apart becomes a real danger when you're too busy elsewhere to keep the home fires burning.

Work

For thousands of couples, work is the main priority, and the one that all too often pushes aside other concerns. Unless you are in business together, most weeks you'll probably spend more waking hours in the company of your colleagues than with your nearest and dearest. Whether you work in an office, factory, shop or school, you'll find the full spectrum of human behaviour on display. There

---

SPEAKING FROM EXPERIENCE

'Clive's work problems really encroached on our marriage. He hated his boss, Charlie, and he would come home and talk on and on about him. Every night it was, "Charlie said this... Charlie did that... You won't believe how Charlie treats so-and-so." Hearing all this endless stuff was getting me down, and it wasn't helping Clive either. In the end I said that he ought to change his job or stop complaining. Moaning on, without trying to do anything to improve things, is a waste of time. He took the point and started negotiating. Now he works from home three days a week and things are hugely better.' LOUISE

---

can't be many members of the workforce who haven't experienced work-related stresses at some stage of their careers.

For most couples, work is a fact of life. They can both expect to be earning for many years, even if one of them, still usually the woman, does take time out for a while to have children. That means you'll need to find, and re-find, a balance between the time you spend at work and the time you have to give to each other.

Workaholics

In every company you'll find those people who put in extra hours, not just occasionally, but day in day out. They're at their desk at crack of dawn, and stay until well after everyone else has gone. Bulging briefcases go home with them, and they never take a holiday unless their lap top comes too. These are workaholics.

If you're married to a workaholic, you can expect to take second place to your partner's job most of the time. Counsellors see this pattern more and more frequently. What's the explanation? Counsellor Ruth Cole believes that, 'Being a workaholic is a way of distracting yourself from anything unpleasant that's going on in the rest of your life. And it stops you having to express fears and anxieties about your relationship because you're simply never there to see what's going wrong or to talk about it.'

REAL LIVES

'He can't hold down a job.'

Carole and Ryan came to Relate because Carole had reached breaking point. 'When we met, Ryan was working in television. He'd had his job for a couple of years and it all seemed fine. But then he had a row with the boss and left. He got another job without too much trouble, and I didn't think much about it. At first this second job was wonderful, he loved it. About this time, we got married. And then it all went pear-shaped again. He stopped liking the job and handed in his notice without another one to go to. That was nearly ten years ago, and the pattern's been the same ever since: get a job, love it, go off it, have a row or resign. Sometimes there's a gap of six months or more before he finds something else. Two years is the most he's stayed anywhere. Meanwhile, although we've got two children under five, I've had to go back to full-time teaching much sooner than I wanted so that we can be sure of having enough of a regular income to pay the mortgage. Although it's fortunate that I have a profession where I can easily find work, I sometimes feel that Ryan is using me, so that he can simply give up whenever the going gets tough.'

Counsellors say: 'The pattern that Ryan established when he was younger, of leaving a job as soon as he gets fed up, needs to change. Carole and Ryan must try to reach an agreement that he won't resign unless he has another job to go to. Carole may well be living with an underlying uncertainty, wondering whether Ryan would ever walk away from their marriage as easily as he discards a job. All their problems revolve around the deep problem of why Ryan can't settle in a job for any length of time. That may stem from deep-seated experiences in the past, and it might only be possible to unravel the reasons through counselling or therapy. If Ryan can work at understanding more about his work motivations, he might be able to find a job that he wants to keep, and strengthen and improve his marriage.'

THE BIG QUESTIONS

How might work problems affect us?

Work is a large part of most people's lives, and job patterns have changed dramatically over recent years. Working from home, short-term contracts, career changes, can all put stress on a relationship. Try out these questions to see how much you know about each other's attitudes towards work.

	Agree	Disagree
• Work is very important in my life.	☐	☐
• I often bring work problems home.	☐	☐
• I don't like my job.	☐	☐
• I respect my partner's work.	☐	☐
• I dislike the kind of work I do and want to change.	☐	☐
• I am following a definite career path.	☐	☐
• I don't have any particular work goals.	☐	☐
• My partner's job is just as important to them as mine is to me.	☐	☐
• If I were made redundant it would		
be a relief.	☐	☐
be devastating.	☐	☐
be a chance to make a new start.	☐	☐
• I don't think I work excessive hours.	☐	☐
• I'm thinking about retiring in the foreseeable future.	☐	☐

Reflect on your answers to these questions. Do they have implications for your relationship? Can you see places where problems could arise?

Sorting Out Priorities

All marriages go through phases when some overriding demand has to take precedence – a family crisis, an illness, work problems, the birth of a child. That's understood and shouldn't present too much of a problem, provided it doesn't go on for too long. Neglect your marriage consistently, though, by denying it a generous helping of your time, and cracks will start to appear.

THE BIG QUESTIONS

What's really important in our lives?

When too many demands are jostling for attention, you'll have to make choices about what's most important. Look through this list and decide how you feel about these ways of spending time. Get your partner to do the same – or try to predict what they would say.

How important is it to:	Top priority	Important but droppable	Totally missable
• Pursue shared interests.	☐	☐	☐
• Pursue separate interests.	☐	☐	☐
• See friends together.	☐	☐	☐
• See friends separately.	☐	☐	☐
• Get to the top at work.	☐	☐	☐
• Have regular holidays.	☐	☐	☐
• Have short breaks together.	☐	☐	☐
• Talk together.	☐	☐	☐
• Go out together.	☐	☐	☐

- Spend time with your children. ☐ ☐ ☐
- Seek new experiences and
  challenges. ☐ ☐ ☐
- See a lot of your families. ☐ ☐ ☐
- Have regular time for total
  chill-out. ☐ ☐ ☐
- Be alone. ☐ ☐ ☐

Now reflect on what you've discovered. If, for instance, you're both high achievers at work, or one of you has a time-consuming interest not shared by the other, where will you find time to be together? Are there many things in your 'Top priority' column that exclude your partner? Is that already a problem, or could it become one? Look for a balance between what you do alone and what is shared.

Getting More Time Together

A relationship is a living, changing entity, and it can't survive on air. Finding time isn't always easy, but it's possible. The following methods, tried and tested by couples under pressure, are useful for squeezing more together-time into the week.

- Plan your week together. Give each other priority, frequently. If necessary, postpone or forgo other activities in favour of spending time with your partner.
- If every moment is accounted for, write some time for yourselves into your diaries. Make it a bare minimum of an hour at least once a week, and make it far longer and more often whenever you possibly can.
- Can't find any give in your packed schedule? Ask yourself a

simple question: what's more important – your work, outside interests, friends, or your marriage? With only a limited number of hours to play with, you must prioritise.

- Having dug up some precious hours, treat them like gold-dust. If you've just one evening a week, don't squander it in front of the box. Talk, touch, give each other your full attention. Shift the furniture if that makes it easier to talk face to face in comfort, or snuggle up on the sofa.

- Get a change of scene together. This is all the more important if you have children. Find a reliable babysitter and go away for weekends, just the two of you – this is a real relationship booster for parents. Make big efforts to do this, even if you can manage it only occasionally.

- Give each other a proper farewell when you part, and a proper greeting when you get back together. Forget the snatched swipe at the cheek, the grunt from the depths of the newspaper. Look at your partner, kiss and touch them, stop what you are doing when they come in, seek them out when you get home.

SPEAKING FROM EXPERIENCE

'I sometimes ask couples who are going through a bad patch to try and smile at each other when they meet – and they come back the following week and haven't even managed to do that. It's a measure of how distanced they've become. Make time for hugs and chats, keep in touch with each other's lives. It's easy to let that kind of contact slide, and it's really difficult to get it back again.'
RELATE COUNSELLOR

- Keep tabs on what each other's day involves. This doesn't mean being paranoid or demanding every last detail. Staying in touch with your partner's life makes them feel valued and cared for. Even if you're not that gripped by the details of a planning meeting or toddler-group session, do your partner the courtesy of listening attentively while they recount their day. Stay connected.
- Spend time every day cherishing each other. A brief phone call, cooking your partner's favourite supper – small gestures like these take next to no time, and build up to make your marriage positively better.
- Make plans for the future. Believe in your relationship as something that will get even better, and make every effort to help that happen.

REAL LIVES

'We were snowed under.'

Charlene and Roger came to Relate because they were arguing constantly. Charlene explained: 'The counsellor asked what we were arguing about, and we both said "Time!" – or rather, the lack of it. We were snowed under, both working, three children, Roger's Open University studies, my part-time teaching course. Plus we were trying to set up a small holiday-let business, and I was doing my widowed mother's shopping for her every week. It had got to the point where one or other of us was out, or on the computer, every single night. We hadn't had sex for weeks – too tired – but neither of us was sleeping well either. The arguments were about silly things. We both felt under so much pressure that if the other made any kind of demand, we cracked. It felt as if our relationship was completely empty.'

Counsellors say: *'Charlene and Roger had put their relationship far too low on their list of priorities. They needed to take a step back to see just how seriously over-committed they'd become. Until this particular phase of their lives, their relationship had been good, but neither of them could handle the current strains. Together we looked at each commitment separately to see where they could reduce the load. By postponing their business start-up, reorganising their studies over a longer time, and getting some outside help in for Charlene's mother, they became able to relax and spend more time together. Once the pressure was lifted, they realised that they still loved and were committed to each other.'*

CHECK IT OUT

The life pie

This exercise can help you to see who's getting the lion's share of your time and who's going short.

Draw a circle to represent a day or week in your life, and divide it up into segments, each one representing the amount of time you give to different areas of your life. Include time for sleeping, working, childcare, hobbies – and your relationship.

How does your relationship portion compare with the time you spend on other things? Does the size of the slice vary or remain constant? Does it look big enough to sustain your relationship as much as you'd like? If not, draw an 'ideal pie' sliced up in a more manageable way. How could you set about achieving this?

> 'To prove his love for her, he climbed the highest mountain,
> swam the deepest ocean and crossed the widest desert. But
> she left him – he was never home.' ALLAN AND BARBARA
> PEASE

Daily Life

Pre-marriage, life as a couple can have something of an edge to it,
perhaps, counsellors suggest, because there's an underlying fear of
impermanence, particularly among couples who haven't lived
together for very long. There's the romance and excitement of
newness, and sex is often very good because there are no other
responsibilities getting in the way. Planning a wedding can carry
you along on a tide of excitement and anticipation, but then the
day dawns when the wedding is over. Marriage starts here.

Being married is about sharing the floor-washing, bill-paying,
workaday side of life, just as much as the holidays and
celebrations. It's all-encompassing nature can be part of the
attraction. Setting off on a journey through life with another
person, warts and all, accepting and accommodating everything
about each other so that you can live harmoniously together – that
takes maturity, and has many rewards.

'Is this it?'

If, though, you'd imagined marriage to be fun, magical and special
all the time, the routine of daily life can come as a rude shock. This
is common especially among younger couples, who have less
experience of relationships, and can result in:

• boredom and apathy.

- jealousy and possessiveness.
- a feeling of 'Is this it?'
- disappointment, and possibly anger, that married life is not the blissful dream of romantic novels and old movies.

Keeping boredom at bay

Feelings like this are not unusual as couples settle down into marriage. They need looking at, though, since if boredom sets in, there's a danger that other relationships will start to seem very attractive. To keep that exciting edge after marriage, counsellors suggest the following:

- Allow yourself to accept that as a married couple you will both get a good proportion of your emotional support from each other. This doesn't mean sacrificing all your independence, but does involve visualising yourselves as a couple, going into the future together.
- Married life needn't be predictable or dull. Some couples are happy to be like two peas in a pod, jogging along to a unvarying routine. For others, stimulation, both individual and shared, is essential to keep the relationship dynamic. Feeling comfortable enough with each other to hold and express different opinions, keeping up with shared and separate interests can help to keep the spark alive.
- Be imaginative and thoughtful about doing things, such as giving gifts or surprises, that lift your relationship out of the humdrum and break the normal routine.
- Interest yourself in your partner's life, and stay in touch with what's important to them.
- See marriage as a journey together through a rich and varied landscape, not an empty plateau.

SPEAKING FROM EXPERIENCE

'For 30 years we've always had a "date night" once a week, booked in the diary sometimes weeks ahead and kept as a top priority by both of us. We do something enjoyable that isn't work for either of us.' BARBIE

'Our marriage hit the buffers when we saw too much of each other – we need time apart doing different things. We can handle quite long separations because we trust each other, and always look forward to being together again.' ANDY

'We can easily start to feel more like flatmates than a couple, so we always have a cuddle and chat last thing, and a cup of tea together before we get up. And we both keep Sundays free, whatever.' JOHNNIE

'My first marriage was bizarre. We both led such busy professional lives that we hardly saw each other except for meals out or the occasional holiday. Outcome, predictably, divorce. With the partner I have now, we have chosen not to live together. I find I don't want my loved one around me all the time, but we do have absolute trust in each other and communicate several times a day by phone or e-mail. It suits us both fine.' JANE

'One thing we missed after the children were born, was going away for weekends. Now, we do a 'child swap' with another family, so each couple gets an occasional break.' TILDA

The Domestic Stuff

Lots of couples have sorted out the issue of who does what around the house by the time they get married because they've already lived together. Marriage is often a time for re-negotiating arrangements, however, and one murky swamp that can stretch your negotiating skills to breaking point is housework. Rows can flare up, not just about who does what, but about how thoroughly domestic tasks get done. Should the washer-upper also wipe down the hob and worktops, for instance? Does vacuuming involve moving the furniture? Do beds need to be made, or is it OK to climb back under the rumpled duvet again at night? People hold strong views on such topics, and marriage often challenges their opinions most painfully. Try these ways to negotiate solutions:

- Be aware of your own world view, and realise that other views can be equally valid.
- Decide which areas are most open for negotiation.

SPEAKING FROM EXPERIENCE

'We've kind of lived together for six years – I say kind of because it's always been a house share, with other people around. When we get married in the summer we'll be moving into a place of our own, alone for the first time. Josh is catastrophically untidy – piles of papers and stuff everywhere, clothes on the floor, that sort of thing. The other people in the house moan about him, but he only has to tidy up one week in four because we work a rota. Things are going to have to change when it's just us, and I don't want to be having loads of rows about it.' NADINE

- Be reasonable, don't blame or shout.
- Don't make a martyr of yourself by doing jobs silently and resentfully.
- Value and appreciate what each of you does in the house.

Influences

Family role models can be powerful influences on your view of who ought to be doing what around the house. Did your dad always pay the bills, your mother always go to the supermarket? If you've been married before, who took the rubbish out, who mowed the lawn? You might find it harder than you think to put all your expectations aside and come up with something different that suits your relationship now.

Men and women still tend to fall into the well-worn traditional roles when it comes to domestic matters. Research shows that women who have children *and* a job still put in far more hours of housework than their partners do. We're talking averages here, of course, so there will be some couples for whom this isn't true. But, by and large, women bear the brunt of running the home on a day-to-day basis, especially once a couple has children.

Sorting out how to get housework done is often connected to decisions about money – whether you should spend hundreds on a fancy vacuum cleaner, for instance. And money, as you can see on pages 107–116, is another hot source of couple disagreements.

'We've been told that one of the biggest causes of rows is over men never putting a new toilet roll on the holder when they finish the old one. Put that in your books, Relate!'
CHRISSIE, BROADLAND 102 LOCAL RADIO

THE BIG QUESTIONS

How shall we share the household stuff?

Look at these questions and answer them together or separately.

- Do you broadly agree on how clean different areas of the house ought to be?
- How tidy are you?
- Is your partner tidier than you, or less tidy?
- Do you hoard things? Does your partner hoard things?
- Are you tolerant of each other's interests and the way they impinge on your home? For instance, is it OK to dismantle a bike engine in the living room, or keep work-out equipment in the bedroom?
- If one of you earns far more than the other, does that let them off doing so much around the house?
- What are your attitudes towards having paid help in the house?

Now check through the following list of domestic tasks. It's by no means definitive, so add or remove items to reflect your own life. If you don't have children yet but are planning to, mark the jobs to do with kids to show the way you think they ought to be shared. Put your initial beside the jobs you think you would definitely do, and tick those that should be shared. Get your partner to do the same.

- General housework – vacuuming, dusting. ☐ ☐
- Keeping the place tidy. ☐ ☐
- Taking rubbish out. ☐ ☐
- Paying the bills. ☐ ☐
- Making financial arrangements, e.g. arranging insurance, direct debits, etc. ☐ ☐
- Cleaning the loo. ☐ ☐

- Cleaning bath and shower. ☐ ☐
- Planning meals. ☐ ☐
- Shopping for food. ☐ ☐
- Cooking meals. ☐ ☐
- Washing up. ☐ ☐
- Changing nappies. ☐ ☐
- Feeding children. ☐ ☐
- Bathing baby. ☐ ☐
- Daily care of children. ☐ ☐
- Packing children's lunch-boxes. ☐ ☐
- Taking children to nursery or school. ☐ ☐
- DIY jobs – putting up shelves, etc. ☐ ☐
- Choosing decor. ☐ ☐
- Decorating. ☐ ☐
- Gardening. ☐ ☐
- Mowing lawn. ☐ ☐
- Dealing with plumbing, electrics, etc. ☐ ☐
- Car maintenance. ☐ ☐
- Cleaning car. ☐ ☐

Discuss the areas where you agree and where you disagree. How closely do your lists match? Are they any places where you are undecided?

REAL LIVES

'I did what I thought a wife should do.'

Rachel was a lecturer, while her husband Dennis worked long hours as a builder. They had two children under ten. Rachel's problem was that Dennis never gave any help in the house. 'I did it all. I saw myself as the all-competent mother, who could work and care for the family and be there for everyone. I ended up exhausted and resentful because Dennis was hardly ever at home, and when he was he'd be sitting there reading the paper, oblivious to the kids, waiting for me to put a meal on the table. When I complained, he got really angry. He said that he worked hard to give us a good standard of living and pay for our holidays, and that I'd no right to expect him to do more. The counsellor helped me to see that I'd been brought up with a very definite idea of what a wife should be – my mother had played a very traditional role and my father never lifted a finger. The difference was that mum didn't work outside the home as well.'

Counsellors say: '*Many women, even those who in theory have a more 21st-century idea about women's roles, often work to a subconscious script that dates back to their family background. They fall into the trap of trying to be what a wife was like in their family, then ten years later they're as angry as hell because this isn't what they really want. Women must be more confident about owning their own needs right from the start, otherwise they will definitely come to grief. Young women are sometimes better at doing this than older ones, but often it makes them very angry, which isn't helpful in getting a good compromise. Couples need to learn to negotiate with each other repeatedly over the years in order, to get what they both want.*'

'*I don't want to hear about ironing. I don't want to smell the iron. Why? I regard it as a badge of servitude.*' MAEVE BINCHY, NOVELIST

Getting the Balance Right

Every couple has to work out their own way of finding a balance that suits them best. Recognise that you do need to think about this actively. Balance tends not to happen by itself. What does happen is that the most demanding aspect of your life, whether it's your job, your toddler or your teenager, swallows up all your hours and all your energy, leaving you with nothing for yourself and your partner. Be aware that this could happen, and you're much better placed to make sure that your relationship gets more than a brief look-in.

THE BIG QUESTIONS

How much time together, how much apart?

This is a conundrum for many couples. Marriage is meant to be about togetherness, but what exactly does togetherness mean? How much of it do you really want, and how much of an individual existence can you have and still be happily married? To try to find some of the answers, and think about whether or not you agree with these statements:

	Agree	Disagree
• My partner should give up their old interests and concentrate on me once we're married.	❑	❑
• I should have some say in my partner's friendships.	❑	❑
• It's OK for me to go out for the evening without my partner:		
• regularly.	❑	❑

- occasionally. ❏ ❏
- It's OK for my partner to go out for the
  evening without me:
  - regularly. ❏ ❏
  - occasionally. ❏ ❏
- We should aim to spend several evenings
  a week together. ❏ ❏
- Diary-planning to give us time to spend
  together is important. ❏ ❏
- Weekends ought to include time for us. ❏ ❏
- We should spend some time as a couple with
  our families. ❏ ❏
- It's OK if one of us wants to see their family
  more often than the other sees theirs. ❏ ❏
- It's fine if my partner goes out with a friend
  of the opposite sex. ❏ ❏
- Talking should be something that just
  happens. Planning for it makes it seem false. ❏ ❏
- It's important to go out together as well as
  staying home. ❏ ❏
- If a couple have children, each parent should
  spend time with them separately. ❏ ❏
- If a couple have children, parents and
  children should frequently do things
  together as a family. ❏ ❏

All these are things that many couples never think about because they automatically respond to whichever demand seems most pressing, without thinking whether there are better or different ways to organise their time. And time, given regularly and ungrudgingly to each other, is one of the most valuable gifts you can give.

REAL LIVES

'There's so little intimacy left.'

Dietmar, 45, and Catherine, 37, are an Anglo-German couple who have been married for four years. They have two under-fives. Dietmar has a high-powered professional life and Catherine is a houseparent, having given up her career in administration to have a family. Catherine says, 'Dietmar is too preoccupied with his career. He is often very late home, or working abroad. He doesn't have much of a relationship with the children because he hardly sees them. When he is home he is tired stressed and irritable. Our sex life is non-existent, too, because I can't bring myself to have sex when there's so little emotional intimacy left between us.'

Counsellors say: *'This couple are in a very precarious situation. It wouldn't take much to push Catherine over the edge into an affair. Catherine needs to tell Dietmar just how serious the problem has become. Although she knows that his career is very important to him, there just has to be a better balance in their lives. If this is too hard to say, she could write it in a letter to him, but it has to be expressed somehow. Dietmar must realise that unless he reduces his commitments and spends more time with his family, there is a real risk of the relationship collapsing. If he refuses to change, then Catherine has to face the fact that he may not value their relationship enough to alter his life. She may be faced with the possibility of separation. Even though this would make her feel vulnerable as she has given up her job, Dietmar would have to support her financially and it would be possible for her to leave if he can't or won't give more of himself to her and the children.'*

Out of the time you spend together talking and sharing different aspects of your lives comes understanding and appreciation of each other. It isn't selfish to give regularly to each other, using time that might otherwise have been given over to, say, your children or your families. Together, a married couple is like the bottom deck of a house of cards. All the other layers depend on you for their stability. If you wobble, everything collapses. That's why it's vital to put effort and energy into being together. Creating a mutually supportive relationship is fulfilling and enjoyable, and well worth the time it takes.

Summary

- Find time for each other every day.
- Don't let work worries come between you and your partner.
- Decide on what's really important to you both, and go for it.
- Get the housework under control and free up more time for fun.
- Say 'no' to too many other commitments, and 'yes' to more time together.

9

Strike a Balance with Family and Friends

Marry, and you become members of each other's families at the same time as you create a new family of your own. With luck, you'll feel instantly at home with your partner's family, and warmly welcomed by them. Even so, it can take time to get used to another family's expectations of you as a married couple, and to accept the way they do things, which might be very different from the way your own family behaves.

How much real effect your families have on you depends on lots of things:
- How near you live.
- How close a relationship you have.
- How well you get on with each other's families.
- How old you are, and how long it is since either of you lived with your family.

THE BIG QUESTIONS

How are we going to get on with our families?

Think about these questions and answer them for yourself and with your partner.

	My Parents	Your Parents
• How often will we see our parents?		
Every day.	☐	☐
Once a week.	☐	☐
Once a month.	☐	☐
On special occasions.	☐	☐
Seldom or never.	☐	☐

- Are there other family members, apart from parents, whom we might see regularly?
- Will either of us see family members alone, or will we always see them together?
- If either of us has family who live a long way away, or even in another country, how will we keep in touch?
- What should remain private between us as a couple, and what is OK to discuss with our families?

	Private	Family
Our plans for children.	☐	☐
Financial matters.	☐	☐
Any worries we might have.	☐	☐
Problems in our relationship.	☐	☐

- Would we be happy to accept financial help from family?
- Is it all right for family members to pop round without calling first? If not, how will we come to an understanding on this?
- What do I like most about my partner's family? And what do I like least?

All these points are very important, but don't worry if you can't reach any conclusions straight away. It takes time for family relationships to settle down after a major change, such as a wedding. Take it one step at a time.

Try to be tolerant of each other's families, and do everything you can to avoid any hostilities building up. These people will be part of your lives for many years to come, and it's in everyone's interests that you develop as harmonious a relationship with them as possible even if that involves you in a lot of compromise.

Your Wedding and Your Families

Families usually get involved – sometimes heavily involved – with wedding plans. It's very important to keep control of your own celebration, and can be a good move to make up your minds what kind of wedding *you* want, then present your plan, tactfully but firmly, to your family.

Talking through the questions below with your partner can highlight some of the trip-wires strung across the wedding route. See pages 20–24 for more about weddings.

- If our parents haven't met already, what would be the best way to arrange this?
- How involved do we want our families to be in organising our wedding?
- How involved will they want to be?
- Who's going to pay for the wedding?
- Is the kind of wedding we want the kind of wedding they would want us to have?
- If we have children, either together or from previous

relationships, how involved are they going to be?

- Are we planning to invite ex-partners?
- If either set of parents is divorced and/or remarried, and
  particularly if they are on bad terms with a former spouse,
  you'd be well advised to ponder on questions such as:
  - Who gives the bride away?
  - Whose name is on the invitations?
  - Who will be in a receiving line?
  - Who will make speeches?
  - What will the seating arrangements be?
  - Who will be included in which photographs?

There are lots of traps when it comes to making arrangements
that keep everyone happy, so be flexible. The earlier you can act to
prevent difficulties, the better. Getting off on the right foot can
help to make strong family relationships later on. People
remember weddings for years to come, and you want yours to be
memorable for all the right reasons, so stick to your ideas of what
you want, but at the same time be as understanding and flexible
as you can.

REAL LIVES

'My mother-in-law took over.'

Katy, 23, came to see a counsellor in a panic three months before
her wedding. 'My fiancé's mother has hijacked our wedding. We
wanted a quiet wedding a couple of years down the line, when we'd
got a house. But Gavin's mum said she'd give us some of her
savings so that we could get married much sooner. Except she
didn't actually hand the money over – she's kept control of the

budget and all the arrangements – drawing up a guest list, ordering a huge cake. But the real problem is the way Gavin's reacting. Instead of telling her to leave off, he says he can't say anything because he doesn't want to hurt her, even though he doesn't want a big wedding any more than I do. When he said it, I had this awful flash of insight: if I marry him, it'll be like marrying his mother. My respect for him died. I'm not marrying a man who can't say no to his mum.'

Counsellors say: 'It's normal for parents to want to be involved, but it should be the couple's day from the word go – you must be in control. This isn't entirely about the wedding, though. A wedding is just a one-day party, but marriage is for life. Katy is right to fear that she'll never be free of her mother-in-law's influence if she marries Gavin. Maybe he can change and win back her respect, but he needs to do it now, before they get married. It's never too late to say no if you have serious second thoughts. Katy didn't want to let people down by cancelling, but after she'd talked things through with me and her own parents, she decided to postpone the wedding until her feelings were clearer.'

People are usually very sensitive about their families. Just as Gavin couldn't say no to his domineering mother, many people can't take hearing any criticism of their own tribe, even if they're creating merry hell. Walk on eggshells when talking to your partner about their family. Think about your own family's views on marriage, and your partner's, and try to take on board the inevitable differences.

Setting the Boundaries

Parents, even well-meaning ones, who don't give a newly married couple enough space to sort out their own lives, can be a big problem, particularly for young marrieds, who find it hard to keep interested mums and dads at arm's length. Just as you need to be in charge of your own wedding arrangements, it's equally important after you are married to set some boundaries as to how much input from families is acceptable. This may have to happen gradually, but happen it must so that you can to make your own lives together in your own way, even if this doesn't always tally with what your families expect. You need to discuss the question, firmly but pleasantly, and try to avoid either side taking umbrage.

One advantage for older couples is that they've had a chance to distance themselves from family influences and establish themselves as separate individuals. They may, however, have to take on board each other's elderly and sometimes demanding or needy parents.

Family Celebrations

Do you look forward to seasonal holiday times when families traditionally gather, or dread them? Any of these festivities, such as Christmas, Passover, other religious festivals, or birthdays can be emotional dynamite, and that's true just as much for long-established couples as for newly-weds.

It can help a lot to think it through before the event, and make some strategy decisions.

- Decide how and where you want to spend the time so that you have an answer ready when people ask.
- Family gatherings can be especially hard for people who are parted from their children because of a divorce. Start

SPEAKING FROM EXPERIENCE

'My wife is very close to her sisters. She tells them everything, I know she does. I've had to get used to it. Now, instead of them coming here, she goes back to her mum's place overnight about once every six weeks, and all the girls get together and have a good old chat. That suits me a lot better than having them here.' PHIL

'My mother-in-law, who is Indian, used to turn up with a half-cooked meal in her own pots and pans, and carry on cooking it at our home. My husband talked to her about it, and now she always asks first. She wants to help, and it would be hurtful to say no.' KRISTIN

'My dad thinks Dave – he's a musician – ought to get a "proper job". We get so much stick from him that we never visit. I've had to choose – Dad or Dave.' MARIE

'The day after we got back from honeymoon, my mother-in-law arrived on the doorstep uninvited and wanted to look at all the wedding presents. My wife couldn't see what the problem was – at her house the back door was always open and people were always in and out, whereas I was brought up believing that you never, never popped in – you always rang first.' JAMES

'My husband rings his widowed mum every night. He shuts himself away and chats for half an hour. I'm jealous of that closeness. He never talks to me like that.' HILS

negotiations early to find a solution, but be willing to put your own needs aside if that is necessary to make things best for the children.

- In some families, giving big presents for Christmas and birthdays is the norm, and if you don't follow the tradition, it is taken as meaning that you don't care. Try to find out what usually happens in your partner's family. If you can't afford very expensive gifts, it might be better to say this in a card, or conversation, rather than keep quiet and risk being misunderstood.
- Lower your expectations. Just because it's a festive time, there's no guarantee of happiness and harmony.
- Step back and say, 'We're in this new situation now'. Create your own family rituals.

Family Rifts

What happens if your family disapproves of your marriage? Most people want their families to be happy about their marriage partner, but there are myriad reasons, typically concerning differences in race, class, age, or just plain personality, why families might struggle to welcome your decision wholeheartedly.

Ultimately, of course, who you marry is up to you, and if your family aren't happy, so be it. Rather than rejecting their objections out of hand, though, first think about them carefully.

'I didn't raise my son to go off and marry someone like her. She's just not good enough.' JACKIE, MOTHER OF FILM STAR SYLVESTER STALLONE

- If your relationship with your family is good, but they persist in disapproving of your partner, could they have a genuine cause for concern? A family who love you will usually swallow their disappointment if they can see that your partner makes you happy.
- If you've had a bad relationship with your family, be sure that you aren't marrying someone they dislike in order to hit back at them.
- Do everything possible to avoid a feud. Counsellor Julia Cole explains why: 'A family rift can drive a couple into each other's arms. It's tempting to say, "We don't need anyone else if we have each other," but people do need their families for all sorts of reasons. Clinging together because your families have rejected you can make you feel closer than you really are. When the storms die down – and usually they do because parents seldom want a separation from their children – the couple may drift apart emotionally because they don't need each other so much. It can be very hard to face this – you've been through so much in order to be together. But relationships that start in the face of family opposition can founder when that opposition is removed.'

Problems Within the Extended Family

The goings-on in the lives of your extended family – parents, siblings and others – can send out shock waves that shake *your* life, too. How much you are involved with your families depends on your closeness, both geographically and emotionally.

CHECK IT OUT

Crisis time in the family

What happens when there's a drama in your family? How much might it affect you?

Your parents

They may be active and well now, but things change.

- What would happen if one parent was ill and the other needed support or practical help?
- When, inevitably, one of your parents dies, how will the other manage? Might they want to live with you? Would you be called upon to help?
- How much support would you want to give? What stage might you be at yourself?

Your brothers and sisters

- How close are you? Would it affect you if a sibling had a relationship break-up?
- What else might happen in your siblings' lives that could have an effect on you?

Ex-partners and children from a former relationship who do not live with you

Although you may not see these people very frequently, events in their lives can still be very influential.

- Suppose your ex could no longer care for the children or moved with them a long way away? See page 171 for more about difficulties with ex-partners.
- What would you do if a child who currently lives elsewhere wanted to move in with you?

These kinds of experience are common, but every family will have its own variations on the kind of crises and turning points that can arise. The purpose of looking at these questions is to reflect on how the uncertainties of other people's lives can precipitate lasting changes in yours too, and to think about what your response and your partner's response might be.

The family web

One way to think about all the different tensions and connections within your family, is to draw a plan of the family like a spider's web. Who's in the middle? Is it you, or is someone else central in your family? How does the central person connect to the others, and how do they connect with each other? One side of the web may have a thick tangle of connections, while the other side has fewer, thinner strands binding the family members together. Who is part of the web? Is there anyone who keeps themselves detached from the family?

Think about your drawing. Where do you fit into the picture? Are you happy with your position in the web? How do you feel about the connections? Are they too tight, or too loose? Is there anything you would like to change? If so, how could you set about shifting the balance?

'His kids intrude too much.'

Alex came to Relate in a fury, demanding crisis counselling. Her husband Jack had two teenagers from his previous marriage, who had decided to move in with them with out notice. 'They rang up last week and said their mum wanted a break – she's studying for a teaching qualification – so they'd like to move in with us for a while. I could hear this conversation going on over the phone, and what amazed me was that Jack said, "Fine, OK". He didn't have the nerve to ask me. They turned up that night in a friend's van with all their music centres and stuff. They've taken over the house, they want meals, their washing done, the lot. Jack just says, "Sorry, but I can't say no – they're my kids". I've told him, "Forget it mate, this is my house too, and I say they go. It's them or me".'

Counsellors say: *'Alex's distress and anger are understandable, but so too are Jack's feelings. He loves his kids, and part of him is pleased that they want to live with him. Where he went wrong is in not talking the ramifications through with Alex before he said yes, getting her agreement, and setting up some ground rules, such as how long his children would stay, what would happen about meals, how much help they would give in the house, etc.*

'Issuing an ultimatum isn't going to help matters, however. A better way forward would be for Jack and Alex to listen to each other and try to understand each other's point of view as they work towards a compromise. Being open about your needs and your fears, without blaming or accusing, is the most productive solution in this kind of situation.

'Re-formed families have unique but not insurmountable

problems. Taking the children's needs into consideration is hard
if you are feeling hurt, but it can help to reduce the anger by
coming at the problem from a different direction, and trying to
see the situation through the children's eyes. Jack and Alex could
sit down with the children and ask them what they feel about
moving in, what would help them, and how they can all try to
make things easier.'

Ex-partners

Since the average couple are both over 30 when they tie the knot,
most people will have a history of previous relationships by the
time they settle down with one partner for good. Whether a
previous relationship ended in separation, divorce or death,
former partners often create lasting vibes which can stir things up
in a new relationship. Even if your partner had a clean break with
their ex and never sees them, the 'ghost' of the ex can still
influence the way things go for you. What's more, if it was your
relationship that caused the break-up of the previous one, then
you could have a very angry, bitter ex on your heels.

There are two strands to the ex factor. One is to do with
children, who too often find themselves used as bargaining tools in
an acrimonious break-up. There are many, many ways that
parents can torment each other via the children, and a new
partner often gets caught up in the flak. Going through a divorce
can involve a huge sense of loss, and having the ex-partner still
around acts as a constant reminder of the bad times, and can
make it much harder to accept the loss and move on from it.

The other ghost-image of a previous relationship shows itself
when patterns of behaviour continue that are no longer appropriate.

Powerful emotions from the past can't be exorcised overnight. It's hard to break old habits, and first you have to know where the old reactions are coming from. Counselling might help here. Christine Northam says, 'Understanding why previous relationships didn't work out is very valuable as it can prevent the same thing happening again. It's only by putting down building blocks in the new relationship, through understanding together what the old problems were, that you can create something better and stronger than what went before.'

CHECK IT OUT

Is an ex-partner creating a problem in our relationship?

Think about the following points, and talk them over if you can.

- Are there difficulties with an ex in sorting out arrangements with the children?
- Are you able to talk amicably to your partner's ex?
- Does your partner's ex pose a threat to your relationship?
- Does your partner ever seem to behave in a way that doesn't 'fit' with your relationship?
- Did your partner's former partner die? How long ago did that happen? Have they really mourned the death and come to terms with it?
- If there is contact with a former partner, how amicable is it?
- What is your view of your partner's ex?

An ex-partner can loom like a genie over a new relationship, especially if they try in any way to control what is going on between you. To get them back inside the lamp, you need to

*understand what the fear is and talk to your partner about how
real it is. Do you think your partner's ex could split you up? Take
the children away for good? Get your partner back?*

Friends

Friendships often change gradually after people are married.
There's less time to keep up with friends, and you may not need
them so much once your life is more settled.

The patterns of how and when you see friends might start to
change. Friendships could cause a problem:

- If one of you keeps up with a pattern of seeing friends – like
  clubbing on a Friday night – that excludes the other.

- If one of you dislikes the other's friends, or has nothing in common with them. This is often more noticeable if you come from different social backgrounds, race or age groups which are reflected in your friendships.
- If one of you is jealous of the other's friendships.

See Resolve Conflict (page 75–93) for ideas on how to work out a compromise about friendships. You should hesitate over giving up on good friends just because they don't get on with your partner. Beware of dropping all your friends so that you're left without their support. Give it time, too. Couples' friendships change naturally as they meet new people together, or if they move home or have children.

REAL LIVES

'My husband is jealous of my friendship.'

Lydia's marriage had reached a crisis because of her husband's ultimatum. 'Last year, when my husband was often away overnight for work, instead of talking to him about how lonely I felt, I turned to a male friend, someone I'd known for years, for support. We can talk about anything, and I feel that he gives me a safe place where I can express my most intimate thoughts without being judged. I can't talk like this to my husband because he overreacts and starts to shout at me. When I can't see or talk to my friend for a day, I feel really sad. But now my husband has found out about my friend and says that I must make our marriage my priority, that he has learned from what has gone wrong and wants to make me happy again, but he can't do it while

I'm preoccupied with someone else. He says he feels neglected and ignored – all the things I used to feel – and he wants me to end the friendship now. I want our marriage to be a success, but not if it means losing my best friend.'

Counsellors say: 'If you want the marriage to be a success, you and your husband will have to work together to make that happen. You cannot continue with your friendship in its present form if you want your marriage to survive. On the other hand, it may be unreasonable for your husband to expect you to drop your friend completely. Your husband must start answering more of your needs, for companionship and someone to talk to, but in turn you must make sure he has nothing to be jealous of by becoming less intimate with your friend and never telling him anything you wouldn't say to your husband. Doing that would put you on very dangerous ground that could lead to the affair your husband undoubtedly fears.'

Aim for Balance

Although once you're married it's your spouse who's likely to be your number one friend and closest family member, you'll still have contact with, and need, other people. Aim to balance the amount you see of family and friends, and the degree of input and influence they have over your life as a couple, so that neither of you feels left out or threatened. That way you can reap the benefit of close family links and good friendships without undermining your marriage.

Summary

- All families are different, and it can take time to slot into each other's comfortably.
- You'll need to set up limits if your families want to over-involve themselves in your lives.
- Make your wedding day as you want it.
- Avoid causing a schism within the family. Be a peace-maker.
- Events in the lives of other family members can affect your lives too.
- Ex-partners can have far-reaching effects on your relationship.
- Friendships often change when a couple marry.

10

Enjoy the Sunshine, Weather the Storms

Every marriage has its high spots and happy times. Every marriage also has its crunches, its crises. Whether you win the lottery or lose your job, move to a mansion or break a leg, the net result is change. Over a lifetime, a whole raft of changes is bound to come your way.

Change is part of living. You shift jobs, have children, go back to college, move house. You hit 30, 40 or 50, your ideas shift and so do your priorities. All these events, and many more besides, have a knock-on effect on both your lives.

Many changes are positive and exciting, but the simple fact that things are no longer predictably the same, even if it's all for the good, can be enough to rock your marriage. For instance, having a baby can mean that you need your partner more, or need them in a different way. Starting a new job can mean you see less of your partner. If one of you is ill, the other might need to take on a different role in the family for a while. You'll need strategies to help you adapt so that you can enjoy the excitement of new horizons, cope well with difficulties, and emerge with your relationship as strong, or stronger, than it was when you started.

REAL LIVES

'Everything in our lives is different now.'

'If you'd asked me when I got married ten years ago where we'd be now, I'd have said we'd still be living in London, have two kids about two years apart, both of us would be fit and well, and Tim would be in the same job. Instead of which, our first child was born on schedule, but then, over the next four years, we had great difficulty conceiving again, two traumatic miscarriages, and, finally a successful second pregnancy, after which I had ghastly post-natal depression, and three months of psychiatric care.

'While all this was going on, Tim's company relocated, totally unexpectedly, and we moved from London to a small town in the sticks. The job didn't work out, we missed city life, and after three years, Tim changed jobs and we moved again.

'As if that wasn't enough, when Tim had been in his new job one month, he was in a car crash and damaged his back. He had two months' sick leave, and wasn't fully fit for another 18 months.

'To cap it all, last year, my father, who was in his 70s but had always been very fit, was diagnosed out of the blue with cancer and died two months later. My mother has now moved to live nearer us, another huge change for us all.

'Believe it or not, the last ten years have also had some very happy moments. Tim and I have had to cling together to get through this lot, and we are much stronger as a couple now. I take nothing for granted any more, nothing. Each day is a gift, and so are all the lovely little things that happen in a day.'   LIBBY

Counsellors say: 'The kind of changes that Libby and Tim have had to face can happen to anyone, and have the potential to draw a couple closer together or push them apart. Illness, moving,

*changing jobs – all of these are stressful events that can leave
people feeling scared and destabilised. It's helpful to try and see
that most changes, even if unwelcome, can eventually bring
benefits and make new ways of life possible. Use periods of
change as time to deepen and strengthen your relationship by
talking about what's happening and how you feel about it, and
working out coping strategies together.'*

How do you respond to change?

How you cope when something big happens in your life depends
partly on the type of person you are. Can you recognise yourself in
any of the descriptions below?

The coper You tackle problems one step at a time, putting a lot
of work into sorting things out, and sticking to your plan of action.
You try not to worry too much about things you can't control, and
accept that your feelings about the change are natural. You stay
calm by telling yourself that you can manage and that things will
be all right in the end.

The wishful thinker You want to go back in time and alter what
has happened. You daydream about everything being different,
think life is very unfair, look for someone to blame and pray for a
miracle to make things better.

The avoider You try to hide your feelings so that no one will
know what's going on inside you. You tend to ignore problems for
as long as you can. You turn to drink or drugs to tide you over, and
may take refuge in sleep.

The support seeker You are glad to accept help and sympathy from friends and family, and seek professional help if necessary. You talk the situation over with someone you trust.

If you are a coper or a support seeker, then you'll probably come through a crisis well. Wishful thinkers and avoiders, on the other hand, may have big difficulties when they come up against change. Reflect on your own and your partner's style of handling change. Do the ways in which you confront change match, or are you likely to be in conflict? You can learn to change your responses, so think about how you might react differently in future.

Making Your Partner Change

On top of coping with changes thrust upon them by the outside world, some people put a massive amount of energy into trying to force their partner to change. Problems in marriage arise if one partner is doing something the other wants to alter, maybe because they find it unacceptable or worrying. So if you both smoke and are happy with the amount you smoke, then you won't argue about it. But if one of you smokes and the other wants it to stop, you will.

Trying to *make* someone change is very hard, and struggling to do it can cast a cloud over the whole of your lives so that even the good times are marred by this perpetual underlying grouse. Arguments about topics such as smoking, drinking or overeating can rumble on for years and seriously undermine your happiness. One partner becomes increasingly anxious about the other, and increasingly frustrated if they refuse to change their behaviour. If your partner steadily puts on weight, develops a smoker's cough

SPEAKING FROM EXPERIENCE

'My husband didn't have a weight problem when we got married, but over the last couple of years he's got really porky. He's gone up two waist sizes in trousers, and a pair he bought recently are straining round his middle. I try to give us healthy food, but it's what he eats away from home that's the cause. He keeps packets of biscuits in his car, and in the garage, so he's always nibbling, and he goes to the canteen at lunchtime and has chips every day. I say he should cut down and take more exercise. Getting fat like that is really bad for his health. He says he's not fat, he's cuddly – he eats because he gets hungry and that I'm nagging. I'm really frightened that he'll have a heart attack. His attitude makes me so cross.' WENDY

or regularly wakes up with a hangover, it is a cause for concern.

The answer? Relationships psychologist Susan Quilliam says it all boils down to power. 'People know if their behaviour is bad for them, so why do they dig their heels in when their partner asks them to change? Because it's a power struggle. These happen a lot in relationships, where, as one partner pushes, the other, instead of knuckling under, pushes back.'

The cycle of one partner nagging while the other digs their heels in creeps up over several years and is a very real threat to that couple's future. Couples who get locked into one power struggle after another wage a constant war of attrition. They're always sniping at each other, but neither one ever gives in. This kind of relationship gradually gets ground down as the love that used to exist between them gets shot to bits in the flying bullets.

Avoiding power struggles

How can you break the cycle of a power struggle, and move your relationship on, both amicably and productively? Here is Susan Quilliam's plan of action.

Ask yourself, 'Is this any of my business?' If, say, you were deciding whether to have another baby or to move to Australia, then of course both of you would have a say. With smaller niggles, it's very easy to get into entrenched positions that destroy the good feeling between you.

- Don't make threats, such as 'If you don't stop smoking, I won't have sex with you any more.' Your partner will feel that you've withdrawn your love, and the pressure you're applying will make them smoke all the more.

- Has your partner made any steps towards changing their behaviour? If so, support them every step of the way.

- If no change is on the horizon, then it's up to you to alter your behaviour. Back off completely and make up your mind that for two weeks you're not going to mention the problem. Tell your partner, 'I love you anyway whatever you do.' By dropping the pressure and reassuring your partner, you leave the way open for them to step back towards you and change of their own free will, rather than because you nagged them into it.

Handling Crisis

Sooner or later, most marriages will come face to face with a crisis. Some marriages withstand the most shattering of blows – the death of a child, life-threatening illness – while others crumble under lesser strains. Exactly *what* your particular crunch involves isn't so important. Much more to the point is *how* you face it together.

> *'The way I see it, if you want the rainbow, you gotta put up with the rain.'* DOLLY PARTON

How well couples cope together in a real crisis depends on many things, some of which may be outside anyone's control. What you can get a handle on, though, is the strength of your relationship, because you can work on that from day one of your life together. Develop the habits of talking, sharing your feelings, facing up to difficulties and overcoming them together, and giving each other consistent support and care. Make opportunities every day to build on your relationship, then if your boat does hit the rocks, you'll have something solid to cling on to.

REAL LIVES

'Our relationship had died.'

Sandra came to Relate on her own, desperate at the state of her 20-year marriage. 'Dan and I had always been so happy with our three daughters. Then, eight years ago, our youngest daughter died of a rare kidney disease. At the time, everyone said how brilliantly we coped. We both carried on working, we cared for the other two girls. On the surface we were amazing. But we never, ever talked about what we felt when Beccy died. Dan threw himself into work from then on, he closed himself off from us. I felt dead inside, I didn't know how to start talking, and he made himself completely inaccessible emotionally. We've carried on like this, but now our other children are leaving home. One's gone, and the other will be off in a couple of months, and there's nothing there between him and me. It's as if our relationship died when Beccy did.'

Counsellors say: *'Traumas as deep as the loss of a child are very threatening to a marriage. It's all so painful to talk about that often one partner responds by withdrawing and the other one then feels totally abandoned and left to cope with their grief alone. For Dan and Sandra the trigger has been their other children leaving home. Soon they'll have to face each other with no 'buffer' in between. After all this time it might prove very hard to unravel their feelings about what happened, and they might need the help of a counsellor to do it.*

'People who talk easily may think they can discuss their feelings easily too. Very often, this isn't so. Around 80 per cent of Relate's work is about improving communication between couples. It's a widespread problem for people, regardless of their age, education or background. Talking about feelings is hard. Despite that, doing it, and doing it often, can be very positive. Keeping feelings secret is like building an invisible wall between you and your partner, which only you can dismantle. It may feel safer to have that wall there to hide behind, but in the long run it serves only to keep you apart.'

Building a strong relationship

Think about your relationship. How strong is it? What is it based on? Can you have fun together, laugh together, as well as being able to take a more serious look at life when you have problems to solve? What are the qualities in your relationship that make it special, and different from ordinary friendships, or family relationships?

The seven tests

As a way of thinking about the strong qualities that every enduring marriage needs, Relate counsellors suggest that you think about your partner in the light of the following questions. There's no need to write anything down, or even to talk about your thoughts if you'd prefer not to. The object is to give you a chance to reflect quietly on how strong and durable your relationship can be.

1. Do I want to share the rest of my life with this person?
2. Does our love give me energy and strength, or does it drain me?
3. Do I respect this person?
4. Do I accept them exactly as they are?
5. Can we admit our mistakes, apologise and forgive each other?
6. Do we have attitudes and interests in common, that make a foundation for friendship?
7. Have we weathered a range of different experiences together?

The relationship strengtheners

An enduring relationship, one that's strong enough to withstand most troubles, doesn't develop without you making it happen. Think about the relationship strengtheners below. Which would you find easy, and which would be harder?

- Give each other time, not only when there's a problem, but every day. Build in time to talk, go out and spend time doing enjoyable things together. People who work shifts or who are in the caring professions need to be particularly vigilant. They can be so busy looking after others that they don't leave enough time or energy for their own relationships.
- A good sex life creates a basis of intimacy and trust in the relationship, which can give a terrific boost in helping you

through the hard times. Pay attention to how well your sex life is faring, and take steps to sort out any problems as soon as they arise. See pages 94–106 for more information about how to do this.

- Prioritise your relationship right from the start. It's not selfish to do this, even if you have children. The stability of your relationship is vital to the future security of your family, so safeguarding and nurturing the bond between you is essential.

- Recognise that different stages of life can put pressure on, but take care not to neglect each other.

- It's up to both of you to keep your relationship topped up with good feelings. One partner can't make all the effort – it has to be shared.

You can't switch a relationship on to automatic, then leave it to look after itself. Your marriage needs you – your time, enthusiasm, interest and commitment. Stop caring for it, and it'll end up like a plant in a dentist's waiting room – dusty, wilting and sad.

THE BIG QUESTIONS

How good are we in a crisis?

Look at this list of things you can do to make changes and crises easier to cope with. How well do you do this? How would you like to be different?

- Anticipate changes and don't resist them. Be flexible and accept that nothing stays the same. Digging your heels in and trying to stop changes happening makes things worse.

- If disaster strikes, don't launch into 'poor me' mode. Raging at life's iniquities, retreating into sulky silence or having a good old whinge doesn't achieve anything, and will drive your partner up the wall.

- Try to look on any crunch as an opportunity to alter things. See it as a challenge rather than a difficulty. Taking a positive approach puts you in the right frame of mind to come up with creative and useful solutions.
- Tackle changes that call for action or decisions by talking together and negotiating a plan that both of you are reasonably happy with.
- Saying 'It's your problem' isn't helpful. Face adversity together. Support each other. Feeling that you can always rely on each other's support is one of the most important aspects of a successful marriage.

Is your partner better at doing some of these things than you are? Does anything need to change to enable you to face problems more constructively? If your relationship is one where it's easy to talk openly, you'll probably cope well with changes. If, though, talking freely is hard or impossible, consider seeking professional help. Strong feelings that are unacknowledged can gnaw away at a relationship and jeopardise its future.

Enjoy the Good Times

Every marriage has its great, feel-good times. Enjoy the happy moments, large and small, to the full, and while you do, think about what it is that makes the good times so great. Is it a sense of closeness and understanding, a feeling of shared delight, the experience of taking time out together, or spending an hour or two in close and companionable silence? Whatever it is that gives you that buzz of pleasure with each other, remind yourselves to keep doing it. The more good times you have, the more great moments you create by being aware of what makes you both feel fulfilled in your marriage, the better placed you'll be to handle the not-so-good times as well.

Every marriage has its bumps, but those can also turn into the growing points, where you mature and become better at dealing with life's ups and downs. There's something to be learnt from every crunch, large or small, and everything you learn will stand you in good stead the next time there's a glitch.

Fostering the good times together and uniting against the hard times, ensures that, no matter how hard the winds of fortune may blow, your marriage will be strong and flexible enough to sway without breaking.

Summary

- Everything changes – that's a given.
- You can learn productive and useful approaches to managing change.
- Invest in your relationship and bad times won't break you.
- Create your own happinesses.
- Tend your marriage and it will see you through thick and thin.

Credits

page 20: Quote about Kay Hammond is from the BBC News website, 29/1/02.

page 39: Quote by Guy Browning, from *Guardian Weekend*, 8/9/01.

page 44: Quote by Guy Browning, from *Guardian Weekend,* 8/9/01.

page 73: Quote by Phyllis Diller, from *365 Reflections on Marriage* (Adams Media Corporation, 1999).

page 75: Quote by Rita Rudner, from *365 Reflections on Marriage* (Adams Media Corporation, 1999).

page 95: Quote by Tracey Cox, from *Hot Sex* (Corgi, 1998).

page 146: Quote by Allan and Barbara Pease, from *Why Men Don't Listen*, Pease Training International Pty Ltd 1999.

Further Help

Organisations

2as1
Tel: 0700 2222 700
e-mail: Info@2as1.net
Website: www.2as1.net
A national organisation primarily representing the black
community in Britain. Information on relationships, and an on-
line Marriage and Relationship Support Services Directory.

Al-Anon
Al-Anon Information Centre
61 Great Dover Street
London SE1 4YF
Tel: 020 7403 0888
Website: www.hexnet.co.uk/alanon/info.html
Offers support and help to the families of problem drinkers
through literature and meetings.

Asian Family Counselling Service
Suite 51, The Lodge
Windmill Place
2-4 Windmill Lane
Southall
Middx UB2 4NJ
Tel/fax: 020 8571 3933
e-mail: afcs99@hotmail.com

AFCS provides marital, family and individual counselling for the
Asian community in the UK. Sessions are held between 10 a.m.
and 5 p.m. Monday to Friday. There is no fee during these hours,
but evening and weekend appointments have a fee on a sliding
scale. An Asian women's mental health support group is held
weekly during term-time.

Care for the Family
Garth House, Leon Avenue
Cardiff CF15 7RG
Tel: 029 2081 1733
e-mail: Care.for.the.Family@cff.org.uk
Website: www.care-for-the-family.org.uk
Christian organisation committed to strengthening family life
and helping those who are hurting because of family break-up.
Events and literature.

Gottman Institute
Website: www.gottman.com
American research organisation, headed by Dr John Gottman,
who specialises in researching what makes marriages succeed or
fail. The website has interesting quizzes and tips, as well as
general reading on relationships.

Issue: The National Fertility Association
114 Lichfield Street
Walsall WS1 1SZ
Tel: 01922 722 888
Website: www.issue.co.uk
Information, guidance, counselling and support for people going
through the infertility maze. See also **MoreToLife**.

Jewish Marriage Council
23 Ravenshurst Avenue
London NW4 4EE
Tel: 020 8203 6311
Provides a confidential counselling service and prepares couples
for marriage.

Marriage Care
(formerly the Catholic Marriage Advisory Council)
Clitherow House
1 Blythe Mews
Blythe Road
London W14 ONW
Tel: 020 7371 1341
e-mail: lucia@marriagecare.org.uk
Website: www.marriagecare.org.uk
Website contains a full directory of Christian counsellors and
support organisations. Marriage Care offers marriage
preparation courses at some centres. Contact Lucia Lyons for
details of dates and venues.

MoreToLife
Tel: 070 500 37905
Website: www.moretolife.co.uk
Help and support for people who are no longer actively purusing
fertility treatment and exploring all that a childless life has to
offer. MoretoLife's outlook is positive, while accepting the need
for people to grieve. *See also* **Issue**.

Parentline Plus
520 Highgate Studios
53-79 Highgate Road
London NW5 1TL
Free helpline: 0808 800 2222
Website: www.parentlineplus.org.uk
Information on many aspects of parenting, including divorce,
separation, new families and stepfamilies.

Relate
Head Office
Herbert Gray College
Little Church Street
Rugby
Warwickshire CV21 3AP
Tel: 0845 456 1310
Website: www.relate.org.uk
Relate offer relationship counselling, sex therapy and family
counselling at local Relate centres. Look in your telephone
directory for details of your nearest centre, ring HQ on the number
above, or check the website. The website also offers advice on
common problems, and you can submit your own personal query
to the Relate Online Consulting Service, and receive a personal
reply. See pages 7–8 for more information. Relate also offer the
Couples Course, for couples who are considering making a
commitment to each other, whether through marrying, living
together or starting a family. See page 9 for more details.
There is a range of Relate books, covering many common problem
areas. Full details are on pages 197-200.

Women's Aid
PO Box 391
Bristol BS99 7WS
Tel (admin): 0117 944 4411
National Domestic Violence Helpline: 08457 023 468
e-mail: web@womensaid.org.uk.
Website: www.womensaid.org.uk
Help and advice for women involved in domestic violence. Details of local refuges are also available from Citizen's Advice Bureaux, The Samaritans, the police and social services. Telephone numbers for all of these will be in your local directory.

Further Reading

This is a short list of useful further reading. See also the list of other Relate titles, opposite.

Guide to Getting It On Paul Joannides (Vermilion, 2001)
Accessible and helpful book on sex.

I'm OK – You're OK Thomas A Harris (Arrow, 1995)
The classic text on transactional analysis, with helpful insights into how to communicate better.

Managing Anger Gael Lindenfield (HarperCollins, 2000)
Useful strategies to help when dealing with anger.

Why Marriages Succeed or Fail, and How You Can Make Yours Last John Gottman (Bloomsbury, 1997)
Interesting insights into why some marriages fare better than others, and tips on how to improve your own relationship.

Will You Still Love Me Tomorrow? How to Find and Keep the Perfect Partner Adrienne Burgess (Vermilion, 2002)
Many insights into compatibility, and the factors that make for happy/unhappy relationships.

Further Reading from Relate

If you have found this book useful, you may be interested in other Relate titles published by Vermilion. These books are available from bookshops, or you can order a copy, using the information on page 201.

After the Affair
Julia Cole, £6.99
After the Affair takes a frank yet sensitive look at the reason why people embark on affairs and the devastating effects on the person who has been betrayed.

Babyshock! Your Relationship Survival Guide
Elizabeth Martyn, £7.99
This book recognises the effects that pregnancy, childbirth and caring for children have on couples. While often pleasurable, these experiences can also place huge strain on the parents' relationship. This book identifies the pressures and provides excellent practical and emotional strategies to help you enjoy parenthood while you continue to nurture your relationship with each other.

Relate Guide to Better Relationships
Sarah Litvinoff, £7.99
Everyone who falls in love hopes that it will be for ever. But the truth is that relationships inevitably change over time. *Better Relationships* looks at the practical steps that you as a couple can take to create a stronger, longer-lasting partnership by using better communication techniques, and learning how to have greater empathy with each other.

Loving Yourself, Loving Another
Julia Cole, £7.99

Whether low self-esteem is due to your personality, upbringing, or adult experiences, it can seriously affect your ability to have satisfying relationships. This book shows what makes people choose a particular partner, and includes advice on how to build strong 'couple esteem' that can help to make yours a healthy and long-lasting relationship.

Moving On
Suzie Hayman, £9.99

This book provides information, advice and practical strategies to help you cope when breaking up with a partner. Areas covered include managing negative feelings, helping children through the difficult process of separation, improving family communications and coping with shared parenting responsibilities.

Relate Guide to Sex in Loving Relationships
Sarah Litvinoff, £7.99

Many otherwise loving couples experience sexual problems and will find this book sympathetic and informative. *Sex in Loving Relationships* also makes essential reading if you are considering or have already started attending psychosexual therapy sessions with Relate. By using the series of practical tasks, quizzes and talking points, this guide can help you to turn a disappointing sex life into a more enjoyable, satisfying experience.

Relate Guide to Starting Again
Sarah Litvinoff, £7.99

When a relationship finishes it can feel like the end of the world – but it is also a new beginning. *Starting Again* can help you to deal with your feelings of separation, grief and recovery, and will help you to start looking to a positive future.

Relate Guide to Staying Together
Susan Quilliam, £7.99

Staying Together offers advice on making your relationship stronger again, by rediscovering what brought you together and helping you to recommit to each other and your relationship. Many couples have difficulties and moments of doubt at some stage of their relationship, and the case histories, quizzes and questionnaires in this book can help you see how it is possible to save a threatened partnership and make it stronger than ever.

Stop Arguing, Start Talking
Susan Quilliam, £6.99

Stop Arguing, Start Talking contains a practical ten-point plan that can help you change your patterns of behaviour and discuss problems rather than row about them. If you are tired of conflict in your relationship and want to improve the way you communicate, this book can help you find the answers.

Relate Guide to Step-Families
Suzie Hayman, £7.99
One in three people find themselves as part of a stepfamily or
second family at some point in their life. This book offers
practical and positive coping strategies for all the people
involved – new parents, established parents, children, the ex,
grandparents.

Available from Vermilion

After the Affair	0091856728	£6.99
Babyshock!	0091856590	£7.99
Better Relationships	0091856701	£7.99
Loving Yourself, Loving Another	0091856760	£7.99
Moving On	0091856256	£9.99
Sex in Loving Relationships	009185668X	£7.99
Starting Again	0091856671	£7.99
Staying Together	009185671X	£7.99
Stop Arguing, Start Talking	0091856698	£6.99
Step-Families	0091856663	£7.99

FREE POST AND PACKING

Overseas customers allow £2.00 per paperback

BY PHONE: 01624 677237

BY POST: Random House Books
C/o Bookpost, PO Box 29, Douglas, Isle of Man, IM99 1BQ

BY FAX: 01624 670923

BY EMAIL: bookshop@enterprise.net

Cheques (payable to Bookpost) and credit cards accepted

Prices and availability subject to change without notice. Allow 28 days for
delivery. When placing your order, please mention if you do not wish to receive
any additional information.

www.randomhouse.co.uk

Index